PROFESSIONAL GROWTH FOR CLERGYMEN

PROFESSIONAL GROWTH FOR CLERGYMEN

THROUGH SUPERVISED TRAINING IN MARRIAGE COUNSELING AND FAMILY PROBLEMS

edited by Robert C. Leslie
& Emily Hartshorne Mudd

Abingdon Press
Nashville ✠ New York

PROFESSIONAL GROWTH FOR CLERGYMEN

Copyright © 1970 by Abingdon Press

ISBN 0-687-34332-1

Library of Congress Catalog Card Number: 72-124755

Chapter IX, "Reality Practice in a Pastoral Counseling Course with Student Supervision," by Robert
A. Nykamp, was originally published in *Theological
Education*, V (Summer, 1969, Supplement 1), and
is reprinted by permission.

Portions of chapter VIII appeared in "Education
in Group Methods: A Working Paper," by Robert
C. Leslie, in *Pastoral Counselor*, V (Winter, 1967),
54-56, and are used by permission.

SET UP, PRINTED, AND BOUND BY THE
PARTHENON PRESS, AT NASHVILLE,
TENNESSEE, UNITED STATES OF AMERICA

CONTENTS

FOREWORD

Kenneth E. Appel

These words by Kenneth E. Appel, M.D., are a condensed state-ment of an address given at the graduation exercises on May 9, 1968, for Fellows of the National Institute of Mental Health Program, "Advanced Training for Teachers of Pastoral Care," Marriage Council of Philadelphia and Division of Family Study in Psychiatry, School of Medicine, University of Pennsylvania. In this statement Dr. Appel has not only described the philosophy in operation at Marriage Council but has also indicated his own lifelong interest in interdisciplinary work and training in the field of mental health. He served on the original committee of physicians and clergymen which founded Marriage Council of Philadelphia in 1932. His distinguished career has included: Professor and Chairman, Department of Psychiatry, University of Penn-sylvania, 1953-62; President, Academy of Religion and Mental Health, 1956-60 President, American Psychiatric Association, 1953-54; Presi-dent, the Joint Commission on Mental Illness and Health, 1956-60.

Marriage Council and the Division of Family Study have offered, in my opinion, one of the most progressive and unique programs of education that I know. To all of us who have been interested in the development of Marriage Council, it has become apparent that marital tensions and family conflicts are frequent sources of medical, psychiatric and social disturbances or illnesses. The illnesses are not just psychiatric, as we have seen it. Thus we have sensed the need for something beyond psychiatry and also beyond medicine. This need has been met by Marriage Council.

The emphasis here has been on the present rather than on the past, on working with problems and differences rather than on symptoms, on working with partners rather than on the one-to-one relationship. It was almost a religion, in the early days of the Marriage Council, that psychiatrists worked only in a one-to-one relationship with a person therapeutically. They didn't consult. They didn't talk with other members of the family. Early efforts at consulting with both the husband and wife developed in this organization, and now have become the practice in group therapy and in family therapy and in much of psychiatry. Here was an experience in this therapeutic unit that was antecedent to a development in psychiatry which now has been generally accepted.

During and before the period of the National Institute of Mental Health Training Grant (1964-69) there was an exploring of interpersonal relationships rather than emphasis on and deep exploration of intrapersonality forces, a dealing with the conscious rather than unconscious processes. There was discussion and exploration and action rather than emphasis on logical presentations, free associations, fantasy and dreams. There was a searching for positive potentials in an individual, a tapping of the creative forces rather than exploring and emphasizing the defective, the defeative, the mistakes, the defensive, the failures in people and in their relationships.

Interpersonal experience with a counselor as well as discussion is now emphasized by Marriage Council; that is to say, the couple experiences in such a relationship something beneath what is said which, it seems to me, is tremendously important in the helping process. Working with all faiths is a regular feature of the program; its selection for an ecumenical National Institute of Mental Health pilot study is a natural. It is scarcely possible to realize how many innovations in theory and practice have been initiated by Marriage Council, practices now accepted as customary.

This search for the creative which Marriage Council carried

8

out in the development of the helping process—this search for the creative, as I understand it—is allied to religion. I think of religion as the devotion, both in aspiration and in action, to principles, forces, organizing and sustaining systems that make for constructive action, whether in the physical world, the social world, or the psychological world. It is called by different names, whether in the Old Testament, whether by Goethe, by Bergson, by Tillich, or by Bernard Shaw. This is a context of belief, of process and action that involves clergy and their effectiveness. Devotion is a part of effective individuals whether they call themselves religious or not. Thus I believe counseling, family life education, and family therapy are areas of important contribution which clergy can make to thousands of individuals, many, many families, and to society.

INTRODUCTION

The dynamics of supervision are often discussed but are seldom demonstrated. This book is designed to demonstrate through clinical data what actually happens in the supervisory process. For clergymen and other counselors who seek to grow professionally, the need for supervised experience is pointed out. For those who are already engaged in supervision, new patterns for stimulating professional growth are suggested.

This book asserts that supervision is a key to the kind of training needed to stimulate professional growth. It describes a training process for clergymen in which supervision is central, a process which stresses a vital involvement of the learner both intellectually and emotionally. It emphasizes that growth in this training process has less to do with the acquiring of knowledge than with the handling of emotional needs. It calls for more than an intellectual exercise, although the intellectual emphasis is never absent. It presents material in such a way that clergymen and others doing counseling may see the value of supervised training. It offers an approach which those already involved in supervision may find stimulating and helpful.

Supervision is not new in the training of clergymen. Field education in seminaries has long stressed the supervisory process, and clinical pastoral education has been carried on for many years by supervising chaplains. The concept of supervision which is introduced here, however, offers an approach different from what has been practiced commonly in theological education. Here is an instance where practice in social work, psychology, and psychiatry has a good deal to contribute to theological education. In the model presented, supervision becomes the vehicle through which the clergyman-trainee's personal needs are discerned as they enhance or impair his effectiveness in counseling. The setting for this training is Marriage Council of Philadelphia, a training agency which has pioneered in the development of marriage counseling as a specialization within the helping professions and in the creation of a new field of family life education. As will become obvious in the pages that follow, supervision has always been at the heart of the training program of this agency.

All the chapters in this book were written by participants in a pilot project called "Advanced Training for Seminary Teachers of Pastoral Care," funded for a five-year period by PHS Training Grant No. T21 MH08546 from the National Institute of Mental Health (NIMH). The assumption of NIMH was that since Americans seeking help tend to turn first to their clergymen (42 percent as compared with 29 percent to general practitioners, 18 percent to psychiatrists or psychologists, and 10 percent to social agencies or marriage counselors),[1] by increasing the professional competence of teachers of clergymen a substantial impact in preventive mental health could be made. Marriage Council of Philadelphia was selected partly because it contained an ongoing marriage and family clinic which would permit the trainees with NIMH fellowships to learn in actual practice how to counsel with troubled individuals, marriage partners, and families. Opportunity was also available to participate dynamically in the leadership of groups in family life education. The clinical material included in this book has come out of four years, 1964-68,

---

[1] *Action for Mental Health* (New York: Basic Books, 1961), p. 103.

in which twenty-five Fellows participated in training under the direction of the staff of Marriage Council of Philadelphia. Identifying names and data from trainees, students, and clients have been modified to preserve anonymity throughout.

Since 1952 Marriage Council of Philadelphia has been affiliated with the University of Pennsylvania, becoming the clinical arm of the Division of Family Study in the Department of Psychiatry of the School of Medicine. In cooperation with the School of Education, clinical courses in marriage counseling and family life education were developed and made available to selected clergymen, social workers, psychologists, psychiatrists, and teachers. Hence, Marriage Council of Philadelphia had already been involved in the training of clergymen when the NIMH grant was instituted in 1964. A continuation grant from NIMH from 1969 to 1972 will enable Marriage Council to continue to offer training to seminary teachers in pastoral care.

Chapter I presents a trainee's subjective reaction to the training process, emphasizing the crucial role of supervision. Chapter II describes and illustrates both theory and practice in supervision, stressing nuclear problems in learning. Chapter III illustrates reality problems in the supervisory process by using actual excerpts from taped supervisory sessions. Chapter IV describes the seminar as a peer group supervisory experience. Chapters V and VI illustrate through case material how two trainees perceived their needs for change as stimulated by supervision and other aspects of the training program. Chapter VII demonstrates the value of supervision in the new field of family life education, with illustrations from two specific training experiences. Chapter VIII deals with theology in action through interpersonal exchange in a student group. Chapter IX describes a form of role-playing in a seminary classroom. Chapter X indicates the wide variety of programs now available throughout the country for continued education of clergymen.

As is indicated by the backgrounds of the editors (trainee and trainer), this book is an interdisciplinary effort in which the clinical education of the clergyman is examined in the light of experience in marriage counseling and family life education. Robert C. Leslie, theological educator, and Emily H. Mudd, pioneer in marriage counseling, have both contributed chapters.

The book was developed by a committee of NIMH Fellows assisted by staff from the pilot project. The committee consisted of Robert A. Nykamp, Chairman; Kenneth W. Breimeier, Kenneth E. Clarke, Walter R. Delamarter, Hilda M. Goodwin, Robert C. Leslie, Barton M. Lloyd, Emily H. Mudd, Thomas J. Pugh, Sylvia R. Sacks, John A. Snyder, and Herbert G. Zerof. Special appreciation is due to Barton M. Lloyd for editorial assistance, and to Mrs. Doris Houpt and Mrs. Clara Ford for the many drafts of typing.

Further details of the NIMH pilot project, written during the fifth year, may be found in a special issue of *Theological Education* (Vol. V, Summer, 1969, Supplement 1). A detailed description and evaluation prepared by Edwin Hutchins, Research Professor of Psychology, Iowa State University, is available through the Division of Family Study, Department of Psychiatry, School of Medicine, University of Pennsylvania, 4025 Chestnut Street, Philadelphia 19104.

ROBERT C. LESLIE

EMILY HARTSHORNE MUDD

1

Clinical Learning by Parish Clergy

Kenneth E. Clarke

Writing as a rector in a parish, Mr. Clarke makes a strong case for the need of the parish clergyman to have a supervised training experience in addition to the usual course of seminary study. He demonstrates what actually goes on in supervision, noting how his individual supervision was supplemented by group reactions in the seminar and by discussion of his family life education experience. He notes especially the need of the clergyman to come to terms with anger.

Of particular interest is the account of marriage counseling with Mr. and Mrs. Payne, in which Mr. Clarke points out specific learning which took place for him. He describes his early tendency toward passivity in counseling, and the positive results which accrued from a more active role of recognizing existing feelings and identifying new patterns of coping.

Kenneth E. Clarke had been a parish minister for twenty years, serving as rector of St. Thomas Church (Episcopal), Terrace Park, Ohio, when he went into training as a NIMH Fellow. Following training he was Visiting Lecturer in Pastoral Theology, Bexley Hall, Kenyon College. Currently he is Director, Marjorie P. Lee Home for the Aged, Cincinnati, and Director of Research and Development for Geriatrics, Diocese of Southern Ohio. He also serves on the Committee for Continuing Education, which fosters training in marriage counseling and family life education for clergy in the diocese.

When I began my training in counseling and family life education at the age of forty-four, I had already been an ordained clergyman for twenty years. I was the rector of a large and affluent parish; yet in some ways the more experienced I became, the more inadequate I felt. What I found myself doing and what seminary had prepared me to do, except for the performance of liturgical duties, were very different things. Of course, I know there are clergy who are content with minding the ecclesiastical store, but I had always entertained the notion that religion should reach people at the "gut" level. By getting into my own guts, the training helped me convert this conviction into practice.

Much seminary education has been and still is academically biased and emotionally deficient. It still assumes that people learn by being told. If it were that simple, the Kingdom would have arrived long ago.

The Intellectual Bias

The results of this intellectual bias are readily identified. First, there is the effect on the clergyman himself. What does education and training which is almost exclusively focused on the conscious mind do to people? Most obviously and most disastrously, it makes them believe this is the way life really is. As psychiatrists often point out, the mind is like an iceberg—less than one third of it shows and over two thirds of it is submerged.

Operating on this faulty premise, that only the upper one third counts, has a marked effect on us. It causes us, for one thing, to entertain highly unrealistic and often fantastic expectations of ourselves. In the case of the clergyman, it tends to make him think he really can and ought to be the walking epitome of the religious ethic he espouses. Faced with such a demand, he either despairs of himself or, by the

16

process of rationalization, cuts the demand down to his own size. The latter is the more common alternative. Many clergy, therefore, are afflicted by a Yahweh complex. They unconsciously identify with the God they proclaim. Cast in this role, they become "answer men," the ones who speak with authority about the dilemmas of life and death. As such, they are once removed from ordinary people. Consider, for example, the statement I read in a weekly parish bulletin: "To the best of my knowledge, in twelve years of performing marriages, none has ended in divorce." Apparently this clergyman hasn't even considered the possibility that some of the marriages he performed may be as adulterous as the affairs that are ordinarily so labeled. In his thinking marriage is good and divorce is bad. But he went further; it is the marriages *he* performed that have not ended in divorce. Poor fellow, what will happen to him when one does?

Secondly, the intellectual bias tends to make its adherents judgmental and distant in their relationships with others. The clergyman who has rigid moralistic expectations of himself imposes these on other people. If he is a fundamentalist, he will be scandalized by anyone who enjoys a cocktail. But such superficial judgments are by no means limited to fundamentalists. Liberal clergy are simply more subtle in exposing their rigidity. A co-trainee, for example, wasn't making any progress with the husband of one of the couples assigned to him for counseling. He said, "I simply can't get him to open up, but I don't have any trouble with his wife." As it happened, the husband was having an affair with a much younger woman. This so offended the counselor's own sense of values that he was unconsciously cutting his client off. The point is not that the counselor's values were wrong, but that he was letting them unduly influence his role as a helping person. By judging the situation moralistically, he blinded himself to the negative interaction between the husband and wife which precipitated the problem they brought to marriage counseling.

Not only marriage counseling but every aspect of the ministry is affected adversely by the intellectual bias. Consider, for example, such pastoral duties as preparation for baptism or confirmation. When parents come asking to have a child baptized, particularly their first, the clergyman naturally tries to help them understand the meaning and purpose of the event. Generally it is safe to assume that the laity are largely ignorant concerning the theological implications of the service. Usually, therefore, the clergyman endeavors, with all the charm and persuasiveness at his disposal, to explain things to them. In other words, even on the intellectual level he is apt to start where he is rather than where they are. And where they are in the formal theological sense is frankly the least important concern. Baptism, as Reuel Howe has pointed out, symbolically portrays the vital role which love, acceptance, and discipline play in our lives.[1] One could, of course, simply lecture about these things. The results in this case are minimal. Parents will listen politely and then just as politely forget the whole business as soon as the festivity is over.

What is the alternative? It is not easy. It is time consuming. It involves really getting to know the parents and helping

[1] Howe, *Man's Need and God's Action* (New York: Seabury Press, 1953), esp. pp. 79-123.

them to recognize the place which love, acceptance, and discipline already play in their own lives. How do they really feel about the new baby? Are they able to acknowledge their negative as well as positive feelings? How do they deal with their anxiety, and how do they express their anger? These questions may not sound theological, but unless they are explored, talking about theology is in the same category as frosting a cake which is lacking half its ingredients.

This same line of thought could be applied to preparation for confirmation, pastoral calling, preaching, administration, etc. In all these areas the clergyman has to be something more than the man with the message, or that message is not going to be heard. But even more important than the message is whether or not something is really happening between him and the people he encounters. Could it be that this is part of the message? After all, as Phillips Brooks said, "Preaching is the bringing of truth through personality." [2]

Self-Awareness Through Supervised Training

When one has operated on the assumption that "I mean what I say and I say what I mean," supervised training comes as a real jolt, for it is based on a very different premise. Following Freud, supervision presumes that consciousness is an exceptional rather than a regular part of the psychic process. More often than not, unless we are well trained, we are unaware of the real meaning of our actions. We like to believe that some things we say and do are without any real significance. No doubt this is the case once in a

[2] Brooks, *Eight Lectures on Preaching* (London: S.P.C.K., 1959) , p. 5.

while, but it is only once in a very great while.

Not too many weeks after I began my training, I found myself one morning in the position of trying to eat my sandwiches in the ten minutes between a seminar and the arrival of a client. Of course the client, Mrs. Mills, arrived early. The sandwiches were gone, but I still had half a cup of coffee. Innocently enough, or so it seemed to me, I asked Mrs. Mills if she would like some coffee. "I'd love it," she said. "'I haven't had anything in my stomach since seven this morning." Since I am the kind of person who has to report all, note of this incident appeared in my dictation of the interview. Much to my irritation, my supervisor pounced on it with all fours. Grinning between his teeth and behind his pipe smoke, he said, "You're trying to put the counseling relationship on a social basis in order to win your client's approval." While my verbal response was controlled, my annoyance was ill concealed. It seemed to me that he was straining gnats. I told him he was psychologizing. He replied, "If you think it's bullshit, why don't you say so?" [3] I did.

Well, was it? As the counseling sessions extended over many weeks it became increasingly apparent that Mrs. Mills was using the time for her own purpose. She resisted conjoint counseling vigorously and frankly said, "I don't want to share my time with that fink. This is the one hour in the week that is all mine." The supervisor stepped into the situation, and after a joint session with the couple in which the supervisor participated, marriage counseling was termi-

---

[3] If the reader is disturbed by the language, he should remember that it often requires shock treatment to get a trainee to face his tendency to intellectualize.

nated with the recommendation that both parties consider the possibility of psychotherapy. Mrs. Mills was an aggressive-hysteric with tremendous unmet dependency needs. During the interviews it was hard to get a word in edgewise. Having been groomed to control my own irritation and anger, I permitted her to unload too freely. But behind the polite and semi-social atmosphere of the interviews lay my own unconscious fear of blowing my top with a woman who was such an unreasonable bitch.

In order to be of maximum help in a counseling relationship, you have to know your own feelings, trust them, and be able to express them for the benefit of the client. When I sat in on the interview that the supervisor conducted with this couple, I was literally aghast at some of the things he said. In retrospect, though, it was evident that he could express himself freely because he wasn't hung up, as I was, with his own hostile feelings toward aggressive-hysterical women.

When it came time to select a book for a reading reaction report, I chose *The Hostile Mind* by Leon Saul. More than half of my group made the same selection. Even after making allowance for the fact that it is short, reads easily, and was given a strong plug by the seminar leader, the choice by so many was certainly more than coincidence.

It seems clear that clergy have a particular need for help in learning how to express their aggressive tendencies positively. It is not hard to understand why. With the exception of the younger generation, the gentle Jesus, meek and mild, is the Christ concept most people cherish. They tend to see their pastor in the same light. He is not supposed to

21

get angry, or at least if he does, he mustn't show it. While outwardly conforming to what is expected of them, many clergy are seething within. As a result, their anger, though disguised, is often expressed inappropriately. They may insist on certain practices which they know are annoying to most of their people, vent their ire in the pulpit, neglect their pastoral duties, make life miserable for the rest of the staff, and become ecclesiastical martinets. Any insight into how one uses this aggressive drive is, then, clearly applicable to every phase of the ministry.

In addition to individual supervision, there was a training seminar where one's counseling was subject to the scrutiny of both the leader and the group. I found this a much more disturbing experience than individual supervision. Generally the relationship between a supervisor and his supervisee develops to the point where there is strong mutual trust and understanding. In a group this is not as easy to come by. One has to expose himself and his work to a leader with whom there is not an ongoing relationship and to his peers who don't want anyone else to look too good lest they appear even worse than they are.

The first case I presented still stands out vividly in my memory. I had worked for some ten weeks with a young couple and really felt that we were making excellent progress. My own supervisor apparently thought so, too. Much to my surprise and chagrin the seminar leader felt quite differently about it. In her opinion I had overlooked the cultural factors involved and was trying to get my clients to act according to white middle-class values. Whether she was right or wrong is really beside the point. The question is, why did her judgment and that of the group bother me so much? It made me quite angry. Later, in discussing this situation with the group supervisor, she said, "I don't see you as a really angry man, but when you feel insecure, you tend to express your anxiety by getting angry." At the moment I resisted the insight, but I didn't forget it. I now know it was quite accurate. Does recognizing it help? Am I able to act differently? Not always certainly, but at least I am more in touch with my anger and am therefore able to use it more constructively.

Naturally, anyone who has this pattern develops certain mechanisms for dealing with it. These mechanisms may serve to avoid the problem, but they also levy their own cost. In my own case I discovered I had been protecting myself, or so I thought, by an overly cautious and tentative approach to people. Initially both the staff and my fellow trainees found me distant and hard to know. This experience reminded me how often parishioners had said, "You are so different now that I have really gotten to know you." And both at Marriage Council and in the parish several people had remarked, "You know, I was really afraid of you at first."

As I see it now, my sixteen-year tenure in one parish was more my own doing than I used to think. My conscious mind kept saying, "You ought to move," but my unconscious, in subtle ways, kept reminding me that I usually do well on the long haul but getting started is difficult. Although there have been job opportunities I would have welcomed had they materialized, I can also see that there were some that did not develop, and some which were declined, because of the static from this inner conflict.

This cautious, self-protective approach showed up also in the academic and routine aspects of my work at Marriage Council, and parallels in the area of parish work are not hard to discover. For example, after several months my supervisor began to raise questions with me about the length and detail of my dictation. I confessed that I wrote all my cases out first and then dictated them. His response was: "You're not really all that bound up, are you? Why don't you just turn on the machine and start talking?" What I thought was being thorough was actually self-protective perfectionism —and it *was* tedious. The comment got to me, and my first reaction was, "If it's off-the-top-of-the-head dictation he wants, that's what I'll give him." But my dictation became more spontaneous and real.

Applying this to the parish setting, I now see my sermon preparation as often being overly laborious. I have nearly always made a complete outline and then prepared a full manuscript before entering the pulpit. Before I finished, I was able to deliver my sermon so that the congregation was seldom conscious that I had a manuscript before me, but the total expenditure of time took a heavy toll on me. Usually it was the time I might have spent relaxing and with the family which suffered.

Not surprisingly, the same message came through in my family life education work. I spent a lot of time and effort reading and preparing talks for the discussion group I led. As it turned out, I didn't use even a third of that material. After the group got moving, I found there was more than enough material being brought out to keep us going almost indefinitely. As our seminar leader had said, "What those people want is you, not what the books say."

After returning to the parish, I found myself hanging much looser to many things, and the results were, I believe, more positive than negative. If the reader thinks I am trying to persuade him that I have completely reversed a lifetime pattern which is rooted deeply in my own intellectual and personality limitations (there are assets, too), then he has missed the point. I am convinced, though, that the enhanced self-awareness that came as a result of training has enabled me to be more comfortable with myself. Moreover, I am freer to express openly and spontaneously a side of myself that is apt to be kept in reserve longer than is necessary.

Developing Helping Skills Through Supervised Training

So far I have dealt primarily with the increased self-understanding which results from training. This is undoubtedly the backbone of any training program. Yet the acquisition of knowledge and the development of skill should not be overlooked.

The clergyman today can hardly avoid becoming involved in a certain amount of counseling. After all, the church, though changing, still has a considerable stake in family life, and families are never without problems.

When trouble develops, very often the clergyman is the first person people turn to. He is apt to be more accessible than other helping persons, and church people feel they have a claim on him. Furthermore, the clergyman's role as a counselor is once again gaining respect.

Let us look, therefore, at one case with which I worked under supervision but which could have easily been presented to me in my parish office. Indeed, the wife's complaint in this case about her husband's absorption in his business is a familiar story to any suburban pastor. In my own parish I made a survey of the problems which cause couples the most difficulty. Among those married between eleven and twenty-one years, "husband's job demands" was rated first by the women and second by the men as a cause of difficulty.

So in this case, the presenting problem according to Mrs. Payne was: "My husband's failure to spend more time with me and the family."

Without training and grounding in the field of psychodynamics one could easily take this problem at face value. I know because I have been caught in that trap. You attempt to help them work out various solutions to what appears to be the problem, but somehow or other these clever and reasonable schemes never get anywhere. Usually the life situation of such people makes their story seem highly plausible. In the case in question, Mr. Payne had recently started his own office in a highly competitive field. In addition, he carried academic responsibilities and was in numerous professional organizations. Both his opportunities and his responsibilities were at a peak point.

One of the first issues I had to deal with was the way these people felt about changing counselors. As my supervisor had anticipated, they said it didn't make any difference to them. But my letting them know I realized that the change wasn't easy drained off any hidden resentment which could have blocked the counseling process. Similarly, I was prepared for Mr. Payne to rationalize his problem on the basis of his heavy workload. After letting him describe his back-breaking schedule, I began, as discussed in supervision, to try to help him see how he used his business to protect himself. "You seem," I remarked, "to enjoy being under this kind of pressure." Both Mr. and Mrs. Payne, interestingly enough, became very defensive. Mrs. Payne said, "You've got to be kidding. That's really out of this world." Rather than debate the point, I acted on insight gained in our seminars and simply replied, "Well, maybe not."

As they talked on, Mr. Payne referred to the way he had handled himself as a single man and the pressure he had felt even when there wasn't much work to be done. I then asked them if they realized what he had been saying. Both looked puzzled. "Apparently, Mr. Payne," I said, "you don't feel you can do anything about the pressure you are under. From the way you describe your earlier life, this does appear to be the way you like it." Once again both were surprised, but there was no further denial. I didn't press this insight, but suggested it might be something which deserved further consideration. A little piece had been chipped away from their defensive armor, and some groundwork laid for successive interviews. This could not have been accomplished had I responded to their defensiveness in kind or tried to do all the clients' work for them.

I had five individual interviews and one joint interview with these people. Though I now feel the joint interview

27

could have been extended, new patterns of relating and coping were initiated which gave both partners a greater sense of fulfillment and satisfaction in their marriage. Apparently there were also benefits to the children.

I will endeavor to further identify some of the learnings and skills involved by sharing with you the way I experienced these two people. Before I started to work with them, my supervisor had asked: "How do you feel about Mr. and Mrs. Payne? What sort of people are they?"

Counselor's perception of Mrs. Payne. From the intake interview, Mrs. Payne came through as a rigid, controlled, and controlling person who was accustomed to masking her feelings behind a facade of efficiency and self-reliance. In my first interview with her I had the feeling that if she hadn't been so controlled and angry she would have cried.

Learning to work with feelings. Learning to work at the feeling level was undoubtedly one of the most helpful insights and skills I acquired in training. So, with Mrs. Payne one of my fundamental objectives was to help her get in touch with her own feelings so that she could become aware of the negative influence of her defensive mechanisms on the marital relationship.

If I had accepted Mrs. Payne's complaints about her husband at face value, we wouldn't have gotten anywhere. Instead, I tried to help her to recognize her own difficulty in expressing affection and warmth. "It does make me feel uncomfortable," she said. From there we moved on to her disguised need for caring and warmth. Her anger, she came to see, was aroused because she was being called upon to give the very thing she wanted so desperately herself.

Perceiving client's defenses. Mrs. Payne's extensive use of denial was most evident in the way she reacted to her husband's affair with another woman. She spoke of it in a detached, what-do-I-care sort of way. When I expressed surprise at this, she replied, "It hurt my ego, that's all." Trusting the feeling tone I was picking up rather than the words which were uttered, I said, "You know, in spite of what you say, I get the feeling that you are really very hurt and angry." The tears began to flow, and we were then able to deal with her responsibility for what had happened. Difficult as it was to acknowledge, she came to see how she had inadvertently furthered her husband's extramarital involvement. Subsequently I learned from Mr. Payne that this had been a very hard session for Mrs. Payne. She had wondered whether she could come back. But he went on to say that after a few days her whole attitude seemed to change. "In fact," he said, "we have had sexual relations for the first time in six months."

One of the most important learnings that is underlined in this instance is the necessity of keeping the focus on the individual's own involvement in the situation. Looking back on my counseling prior to training, I now recognize that I was much too prone to listen passively while the party before me unloaded all his or her complaints about the other.

Counselor's perception of Mr. Payne. Unlike his wife, Mr. Payne verbalized easily and had a warm and friendly manner. Yet I had the feeling that his apparent openness and readiness to assume blame were really ways he kept people from getting too close to him. It was almost as if he had said, "See, I've told you everything, so don't ask me any questions." I sensed, too, that underneath his driving ambition and perfectionism he had strong dependency needs which he neither admitted nor asked to have met in a realistic way. Mr. Payne did not find it easy to look at these aspects of himself and their effect on his family situation.

Dealing with hostility. In the next interview he was initially quite resistant and evasive. He expressed his resistance by raising questions about the counseling process. Here again I dealt with the feeling behind the question rather than the question itself. "I suspect," I said, "that some of the comments I made last time seemed rather judgmental and that you are wondering whether the counseling is going to be helpful." Though he denied this, the feeling was out in the open. Using his relationship with me as an example, I observed that he did seem to have difficulty in expressing his feelings. This led to his telling me how upset he became over his wife's "reward and punishment" way of treating him. "I never know when the ax is going to fall," he said. After Mr. Payne was helped to get in touch with his own anger, it was possible for him to see how his habit of tuning his wife out contributed to her system of reward and punishment.

Underlying dynamics. In telling of his extramarital involvement, he gave the impression that it had happened almost without his knowing it. Here, as in the case of his workload, he presented himself as victimized. It was significant, I felt, that this discussion occurred immediately after his reference to Mrs. Payne's use of sexual denial as a means of punishment. In considering his extramarital activity I had the feeling that he was:

a. using it as a means of punishing Mrs. Payne;
b. inviting Mrs. Payne's intervention;
c. following his usual pattern of making things worse in the hope they might become better;
d. asking for punishment.

The situation was explored in this light, and Mr. Payne was apparently able to see it as part and parcel of a self-defeating pattern. In all this, as with Mrs. Payne, the interpersonal problems were consistently dealt with in the light of their contribution to and bearing on the interpersonal difficulties of the marital relationship. The not uncommon interactional configuration indicated the mating of an aggressive, controlling, but dependent female with a passive-aggressive, withholding, and evasive male. Both felt that they received significant help which resulted in a more gratifying way of life.

Crisis Intervention

Intelligent referral in crisis is one of the clergyman's most important and helpful functions in the community. Not only marital difficulties but emotional and mental problems of all kinds come to his attention. Before I went into training, a young wife who was in a state of depression came to me for help. I recognized the symptoms and tried to get her to agree to see her physician. That night she attempted suicide.

After I returned from my nine months of training, I was again confronted with a similar crisis. I had learned that suicidal threats are not simply a matter of referral. Drs. Goldberg and Mudd give specific suggestions for dealing with such situations.[4] Following their advice, I asked:

Are you feeling so bad that you have contemplated suicide?
Do you think about it often?
Have you considered what you would do?
Is there anything that stands in your way?

The point is, I had learned that I need not be afraid of implanting the idea of suicide in this person's mind. His answers gave a positive indication of suicide. It was not easy to persuade the family that immediate action was essential, or to find an available psychiatrist, but as subsequent hospitalization indicated, any other course of action might have been disastrous.

The clergyman has been called "the man in the middle." This is often where he finds himself—between a person in distress and the source of help that is needed. My plea is that more and more clergy will be able to utilize their middle position by becoming saving links between the distressed and the professional help they require.

[4] Martin Goldberg and Emily H. Mudd, in *Suicidal Behavior: Diagnosis and Management,* H. L. P. Resnik, ed. (Boston: Little, Brown, 1968), chap. I.

The Clergyman's Identity

The Christian clergyman is called to proclaim the gospel, the Good News. But the day is long past, if it ever was, when all he needed was a Bible under his arm and good intentions in his heart. Recognizing this, the church has, for the most part, insisted on high academic standards for its ordained clergy. Normally this involves four years of college and three years of theological education. As I indicated at the outset, I was driven by a sense of my own need to seek further training. The need I felt is, I believe, a common one among clergy today. Reinhold Niebuhr once said that when he visited a modern hospital with all its shiny scientific equipment and bustling, efficient white-clad staff, it made him feel like an ancient medicine man who had suddenly been transplanted into the twentieth century. Today one doesn't have to visit the hospital to get this feeling.

The clergyman is confronted on every side by social workers, psychiatrists, psychologists, sociologists, and guidance counselors who have training and expertise in the field of human relations. In order to hold his head up and serve as a team member among the helping professions, he must be given the knowledge, the skill, and the training which is common to other professions. And this, of course, is not primarily for his own benefit but for the sake of those whom he seeks to serve. As someone once said, "Everyone is a problem, or lives with one." Trying to give answers to people who can't hear, clergy preach the gospel of love to those who haven't learned the language of love. Therefore, in addition to enabling the clergyman to be an effective helping person, training opens the door for in-depth theological dialogue.

In the case of Mr. and Mrs. Payne, for example, Mrs. Payne was able to release some of her control over both things and people and Mr. Payne stopped using his business as a means of escape and self-justification. A new world began to open up for both of them. At one point Mrs. Payne remarked, "I think I'm becoming a sloppy housekeeper and it doesn't worry me." (Of course, she never will be.) And Mr. Payne said, "Since I've been home more I have found that even drinking a cup of coffee can be fun. I'm seeing things I never noticed before." In theological language, they had relinquished the need to justify themselves and discovered the meaning of grace. They were ready to use the language of love, to hear the Good News.

Leon Saul describes the goal: "The ideal situation is for each individual to be so mature that he understands his own motivations and those of others realistically and has humanitarian feeling not only for himself and his family, but for all people." [5]

The church through its clergy and its parishes still has a unique opportunity to implement this goal. And as I see it, supervised training in working in helping relationships is an absolutely fundamental step toward its realization.

[5] *The Hostile Mind* (New York: Random House, 1956), p. 135.

2

Supervision as a Catalyst for Growth

Hilda M. Goodwin

A major contribution of the supervisory process is the identification of the trainee's nuclear problem. Dr. Goodwin points out how learning is obstructed by the nuclear problem, the problem that is more related to personality needs than to level of knowledge. She illustrates how nuclear problems may be recognized and demonstrates from actual supervisory sessions how they can be dealt with. Of particular interest are the summaries of supervision centering in two counseling cases (the Williamses and the Kirbys).

Dr. Goodwin notes the strong resistance evoked in the trainee by a challenge to change, even when change, in the sense of growth, is desired. She notes, too, the special problems that face the supervisor.

Hilda M. Goodwin was a staff member for sixteen years in the counseling training program at Marriage Council of Philadelphia (1952-68). As chief supervisor of interdisciplinary mental health personnel for the last seven of these years, Dr. Goodwin has exercised a major influence over trainees. Her position as Assistant Professor of Family Study in Psychiatry, School of Medicine, University of Pennsylvania (1963-69), culminated her years of experience in psychiatric social work.

"Of all people I know, I find myself to be the most elusive." This statement made toward the end of the training year by a very perceptive trainee illuminates the rationale for a supervisory process for those who plan to work in the helping professions. Individual supervision of the trainees' direct counseling with clients is, in many ways, the most important part of a counseling practicum. In a recent study, trainees who had earlier completed training were asked to evaluate the various elements in the learning situation in terms of their relative effectiveness. Supervision was ranked as the single most important element.

The Supervisory Relationship

Supervision is a mutually cooperative helping process to which both the supervisor and the trainee bring strengths, knowledge, problems, and experience. It is essentially democratic. The supervisor's authority rests on the basis of his additional knowledge and experience, and on his capacity to facilitate the trainee's growth process. Unity in the supervisory process rests on the commitment of each person to the same goals: greater competence for the trainee and adequate help for the troubled person.

The essential purpose of the supervisory relationship is to help the trainee differentiate between his problems with lack of knowledge and/or counseling skills and his essential learning problem. The trainee's essential learning problem is expressed in his idiosyncratic, automatic, and at times inappropriate ways of feeling, thinking, and responding while counseling.

Knowledge, skill, patience, and commitment are requirements of the person who hopes to deal with the difficult and intimate problems of troubled people. Most important of all is a disciplined self-awareness on the part of the helping person. But self-awareness is not easily come by, even though intellectually one is sure that he is committed to this process.

Part of the supervisory function is the creation of a climate which facilitates the trainee's capacity to know himself and his own motivations more clearly. A trainee defines a typical reaction to the learning process and one of the blocks toward development of greater competence and skill:

> Probably the most painful part of this kind of learning experience is coming to recognize how one's own attitudes, feelings, and prejudices interfere with the counseling process. After two years of supervised clinical experience, I cannot say that I did not know what to expect, but I still found myself defending against the learning in a characteristic way.

Learning that involves change necessitates the giving up of familiar ways of acting and responding and a willingness to live through an uncomfortable period of "unknowing." The trainee must act before he knows what is expected and before he is competent in the new situation. He is under pressure from demands of the new learning situation, but equally from his own demands on himself for "success" and his need to keep his self-image intact. It is through the supportive relationship with the supervisor that the trainee is enabled to feel more comfortable in viewing his own performance and moving through the difficult process of attaining greater self-awareness.

Focus and Content

The focus in supervision is on helping the trainee to deepen his understanding of the dynamics of personality and of the reciprocal interaction of the marital pair with each other and with him. It is not merely lack of knowledge or of counseling techniques and processes that is involved. If this were so, these could be learned through appropriate didactic teaching.

Each trainee brings his own unique set of values, biases, attitudes, and automatic patterns of relating. Each client also brings his own problems and ways of trying to meet his needs. These, plus the trainee's reactions and responses as he attempts to help the client, and his interpersonal relationship with his peers and the supervisor, become the content through which the learning process takes place. An effort is made to help him develop an understanding of what can be worked with in counseling clients, why it works, and how his reactions and responses either further or retard the client's process of change or growth. Generic principles underlying the helping process are highlighted so that the trainee may be able to transfer learning from one situation to another. The trainee is helped to become conscious of his intuitive feelings and responses, so that they, too, may be available for use in understanding others and himself.

The Supervisor as a Catalyst

A major responsibility of the supervisor is to discern early in training the nature of the trainee's difficulties in counseling. If his difficulty is lack of knowledge or of understanding of the client's dynamics and interactions, the supervisor is responsible for direct teaching related to clients and case situations and for referral to reading or other resources.

If, after appropriate knowledge is supplied, the trainee persists in nontherapeutic functioning, the supervisor is responsible for helping him to become aware of unrecognized feelings or attitudes that he may have toward the client or his situation. Should inappropriate behavior persist, it is possible that the trainee, out of anxiety evoked by the situation, is reacting unconsciously in a patterned way to the current situation as if it were the past. In this connection Leon Saul states: "Each adult's place in life evokes from him various reactions in accord with his nuclear pattern." [1] The phrase "nuclear pattern" refers to the trainee's patterns of automatic reaction as a defense against the anxiety engendered by unconscious conflicts, fears, and needs which developed in childhood and which are inappropriate in the current situation.

An understanding and compassionate appraisal within the supervisory relationship of the trainee's inappropriate responses and reactions may enable him to begin to recognize previously hidden or denied conflictual attitudes that block his counseling effectiveness. As the trainee begins to perceive that his problem in reacting realistically and appropriately to clients is related to his nuclear pattern for handling his own fears and anxieties, he may, through reflecting upon these, set in motion a process of growth.

The emotional impact of this kind of learning is often quite poignant and may be a critical incident in the trainee's growth. In reality, the trainee has begun to feel more comfortable and accepting of his own fallibility, and therefore

[1] Saul, *Technic and Practice of Psychoanalysis* (Philadelphia: J. B. Lippincott, 1958), p. 29.

has less anxiety and need to defend himself. It is this that enables him to "hear" the supervisory comments and to allow his conflictual feeling and anxieties to move closer to his emotional and intellectual awareness. One trainee, in reviewing the relationship of the supervisory process to developing self-awareness and growth, wrote in detail as follows:

My first feeling concerning my "nuclear problem" in learning was that my conflict was a feeling of inadequacy which had as its cause an overdemanding need for the approval of others and a consequent avoidance of hurting others.

However, after further reflection upon a case it appeared that the nuclear problem was a feeling of inadequacy as a man—a lack of secure identity—and a consequent sense of self-worthlessness.

The anxiety activated by this conflict evoked defensive mechanisms, some obvious, others not so obvious—but all of them operating to block, when there wasn't awareness of them, a maximum use of self in the helping relationship.

The most prominent defense was intellectualization, which clearly operated in a relationship with a man who seemed to exhibit a weak masculine identity and/or who manifested certain feminine qualities. If the inadequate man defended himself by a reaction formation of superficial manliness—a blustering attitude or exhibitionistic athletic prowess—I reacted by feelings of exploitation and hostility—in an intellectualized way. The intellectualization defense also included a tentativeness, so that every

40

comment in counseling was hedged around with protective qualifications.

The "critical learning incident" which provided the occasion for my awareness of these defenses and their "nuclear" roots took place in the supervision of a marital counseling case.

Mr. and Mrs. Williams both felt personally inadequate and created a pattern of marital interaction in line with their own insecurity about themselves. Mrs. Williams was a rigid, castrating woman who used passive-aggressive behavior to deal with the domination of her husband. Mr. Williams gave every appearance of a successful, aggressive salesman, but his blustery, jocular, domineering exterior cloaked feelings about his own masculinity. His athletic activities—consistent weekly handball and constant attendance at his son's athletic practices—might also have been interpreted as a reaction formation against some feminine qualities. Both parties related in an intellectual way in counseling.

The supervisor commented on my constant use of intellectualization in the counseling interviews with this couple. At first I was aware of negative feelings toward Mr. Williams' blustery laughter which made me ill at ease. The laughter also threatened me because it seemed calculated to control or to avoid. My response to my anxious feelings was to respond in kind to the laughter and not to deal with the possible control. Instead I focused on the intellectual and reflected Mr. Williams' projections of the marital difficulty onto his wife.

41

Therefore, in the initial stages of counseling and supervision I had feelings of dislike for this man. I also felt at a loss as to how to deal with him and settled on this common ground of shared intellectualization. The supervisor continued to point out this defense of intellectualizing plus added information that underneath this man had troubles with his own male identity. I accepted the explanation of inadequacy but did not see how it set me off or what it meant for me. At this time the supervisor raised questions about how I felt about myself, indicating that I used myself in a largely negative way —the "suffering servant"—and did not claim my own strength. I was challenged to find the background situation which created this rejection of self.

At first my explanation to myself centered about rejection by my mother. This seemed to make sense in view of my awareness of the control and rigidity of Mrs. Williams.

Only secondarily and with reluctance did I say (to myself) that I resented my father for being weak. All I could say to the supervisor was that Mr. Williams' sales-pitch approach was familiar to me from my background.

Upon reflection, supervision on this case enabled me to break through this defensive intellectualization and started the process of self-awareness about the feelings Mr. Williams aroused in me. I began to realize now that his blustery manner not only reminded me somewhat of my father, but his deeper insecurity about male identity activated my own feelings of insecurity about male identity. The threat was somehow operating at that deeper level.

In the final analysis the supervisory relationship concerning this couple provided a learning climate in supervision whereby through my counseling with this couple I was able to reach beyond my anxiety, and my defense against that anxiety, to explore my own feelings of insecurity about maleness and self-worth. Subsequent supervision has sharpened this awareness and helped me to a clearer perception of my own strengths.

The Trainee's Commitment in Supervision

Obviously, nothing constructive can occur within the supervisory relationship unless the trainee is willing and able to commit himself to a learning process. This commitment places the supervisor, who will work cooperatively with the trainee to achieve his desired goals, in the role of the catalyst. It is the reciprocal interaction between the trainee and the supervisor which is the vehicle that carries the process of change. Self-exploration has been shown to be related predictably to personality change in therapeutic work with patients. It may be assumed that the same process holds for the trainee who is able to explore and understand his own reactions both in counseling and in supervision. These factors become the focus of the supervisory conference as they affect adversely the trainee's work with clients. The trainee who is able to utilize this kind of help is precipitated into reflection upon his performance and begins the process of growth. Statements such as the following result:

I can see now how many times, because of my feelings of inferiority and inadequacy, I tried to demonstrate my superiority by a reaction formation of overemphasis and overcompensation, thus establishing a pattern of behavior . . . directly opposed to a strong unconscious conflict.

I need to be a nice guy—I want to be liked; I fear and don't want to be rejected. I fear losing clients so I "pussy-foot" too much because of my anxiety. It is hard for me to end an interview without a little word of encouragement—yet I realize now that I have really been trying to allay my own anxiety.

Growth once set in motion may continue, as indicated by a trainee who found the training year difficult but eventually rewarding.

During the year and one-half which has elapsed since training, a process has continued which was begun through various confrontational experiences in supervision. The program and the confrontation with my problems in relating (particularly my tendency to keep my distance in relationship by staying very busy) elevated my level of anxiety about my way of functioning. These experiences and the threat to my self-image produced a need to continue the process of struggle with myself, my relationships, and my self-image. The relevant point is that it was the confrontational aspects of this training which began the process which has continued to pay off. The process has been painful, but rewarding from the standpoint of personal values and interpersonal relationships.

The Individualized Nature of the Training Experience

Each learning situation is highly individualized for the trainee and the supervisor. Each trainee brings his own unique personality dynamics and patterns, his background of knowledge and experience, and his specific reactions to his clients, to the supervisor, and to the learning situation. This is equally true of the supervisor. Thus, the learning situation involves two persons relating to and reacting to each other directly. Each is also relating to and reacting to the learning tasks posed by the clients' situations. This uniqueness is expressed by a trainee:

> For me, it was another new situation. I found myself approaching it tentatively, cautiously. Why? Because I become anxious in a new learning situation and my anxiety it apt to express itself in the form of anger. It is not the new situations which bother me, but new situations where I feel uncertain about what is expected and what I have to offer.

Resistances to Use of Supervisory Relationship

Responsibility for use of the relationship to effect change ultimately rests with the trainee. The essential qualities that facilitate change in the trainee are the supervisor's empathic understanding, unconditional acceptance of and respect for the trainee, and his self-congruence. The use the trainee may make of these is limited by factors within his own personality dynamics and experiences and the two-way interpersonal relationship between him and the supervisor.

The same problem the trainee experiences in relating therapeutically to clients may also be reflected in his relationship to peers and to the supervisor. In some instances the trainee's problem may be resistance to moving into the learning role. His resistance arises out of his feeling that he will be exposing his weaknesses and dilemmas to another person; supervision is viewed as an authority situation rather than a teaching-learning alliance.

It is important for the supervisor to differentiate between the transitory anxiety natural to moving into a new role and the defenses that will interfere with learning. Equally important is the supervisor's capacity to scrutinize his own feelings and attitudes to determine how much these are operative in the trainee's problem, and to be willing to recognize these with the trainee.

This type of difficulty is expressed graphically by one trainee in his half-year self-evaluation:

My problem is related to feeling that I am somewhat "all wise" and expecting others to recognize this in me. In relationship to clients this reveals itself in being benevolent and all giving, and in my own need to have them like me. In supervision it revealed itself in being unable to handle any questions or evaluations about my work. Underneath I would often feel rage, but instead of han-

46

dling this openly, my need to be liked would intervene and often I would be outwardly ingratiating. The supervisor indicated understanding of the anger and the fear of rejection involved in this mechanism. This enabled me to begin to face my need to be omnipotent with clients and the underlying fear that I might be found wanting.

All learning that involves both intellectual and emotional factors is anxiety producing, and the anxiety is expressed in various forms of resistance.

I experienced anxiety derived from several sources—the threat of closeness, the recognition of the need to change from a protected posture (teacher) to a more vulnerable one, and the anxiety resulting from a resonance with the other person's anxiety. Defenses in early months included busyness, detachment, and intellectualization.

Anxiety was most noticeable as I approached a quite new orientation to working with people in distress. . . . The close supervisory relationship was a new experience. I feared the exposure of my inadequacies. What I did was accept the experience passively until I realized it was a valuable learning experience.

Often beneath the resistance is the trainee's fear of inability to change or of his capacity to become adequate to his own professional standards. He may attempt to control the supervisory process in various ways:

I am conservative and pragmatic. I am willing to stay

with tested methods that worked for me rather than try
new things that in time might prove helpful.

In the above instance the trainee is justifying his resistance
to change by his skepticism concerning the validity of this
particular therapeutic method of counseling and is not risk-
ing anything.

The supervisor needs to be aware of his own reactions
to trainee resistances and be able to take them in stride. The
trainee should be assisted to express negative feelings, dis-
agreements, or criticisms of the supervision without fear of
retaliation. It is important where resistances are high that
the supervisor evaluate the current demands placed on the
trainee and where possible temper the demand to the
trainee's current capacities. The following are further examples of trainees' resistance to involvement in learning:

> The problem is that I do not connect with my emotions
> or feelings. Several people have given me different slants
> on this—all of which help me close in on what is meant.
> Someone said that it happens because of all the condition-
> ing to an intellectual approach. Intellectual approaches
> have worked for me—and are appropriate to my academic
> work—therefore, why shouldn't I prefer an intellectual
> manner? Someone else has told me that the breakdown
> is particularly with negative emotions. I back away from
> expressions of anger.

> An intellectual approach to a problem, to a learning
> situation, is a defense with me because it allows me to go
> into an area of unknown with my most elastic abilities

facing forward. With my intellect I can grasp, boil down, distill the problem without ever really coming into contact with it. As a *mind* I am engaged in the problem; as a *whole person* I am not.

In some instances resistance within the counseling situation may be related to unresolved conflicts concerning sexual aspects of behavior.

In the following instance the trainee, Mr. Z., had been very resistant to any suggestions or comments made by the supervisor concerning his counseling methods. Much of his anxiety was related to his fear that he might be caught in a "goof"; and, as he put it, "After all, with all my past achievements, how could I be anything but good?" The trainee's moment of truth, as he called it, came following the interview with a client whose case is summarized as follows:

Mr. and Mrs. Kirby were a young couple who had been married five years, were college educated, had two children, and in many areas of life were quite compatible. Mrs. Kirby complained that Mr. Kirby bought *Playboy* and, according to her, had an inordinate interest in things sexual. Mr. Kirby was reviewing the history of the courtship and marital relationship, describing his way of withdrawing into silence when conflict occurred, while his wife moved out into verbal attack.

The trainee's case notes follow:

There was a rather extended period of silence when it was obvious that Mr. Kirby was struggling in an effort to bring out some very troubling material. He began by saying that he knew it was not all his wife's problems, but he felt the need to prove something too. "I try to tell her about my work but she just doesn't understand. It has to do with my fight to be a man. I know I can do it at work, but I have trouble being a man at home." Mr. Kirby slouched down in his chair, repeating, "It's hard to express." With a sense of exhaustion he said, "Frankly, sometimes I am concerned that I may become a homosexual." Counselor did not respond immediately—felt a bit taken back myself and had real question how to deal with this. My response, after a considerable length of time, was that I knew this was a painful thing for him to deal with, and we could explore it further at a later time.

The trainee was extremely anxious as we began discussion of this interview. He expressed great shock that he had been unaware of his own unresolved feelings in the area of homosexuality. He had been very sure that he had worked through any prejudice he might have in this area. As we looked together at his feelings about it, Mr. Z. shared some of his adolescent experiences in the sexual area and his extreme punishment from a rigid grandfather, with whom he was living. After discussion of the client's probable fears and possible psychodynamics, of how he might pick this up and help the client with it, Mr. Z. was very relieved. He could admit that this was related to his basic learning problem, i. e., that he has always struggled with unresolved fear of authority and a self-imposed expectation that he had to perform at an "A" level to gain acceptance. For this reason, any tentative suggestion by the supervisor concerning counseling skills was met with hidden anger and an assurance that he knew all this from his prior experience. It was in this situation, as he came face to face with an unresolved feeling in the client which evoked his own anxiety to an extreme state, that he was able to break through and permit himself to reopen his channel of learning. As Mr. Z. expressed it:

For the first time in my career, I began to realize that there were considerable unresolved feelings to which I could not admit. . . . Later I used this case material in a clinical training conference, at which time the mirrored reflections of others in the group helped to further clarify and define the interactional nature of the marital problem.

Every trainee experiences anxiety which may cause psychologically defensive maneuvers and temporarily interfere with his capacity to function effectively. Anxieties of exceptionally creative people in a training situation may take the form of an apprehensive sensitivity. One such trainee wrote:

Fantasy has always been a major defense with me. My world has been peopled with heroes rather than anti-heroes. . . . My ego ideal is high. I am a perfectionist, but only in the realm of relationships. I have to know the answers, but only as a means of fulfilling my role in life. I have to know all about a situation, how to deal with it and control it and do it with spectacular success, before I move to get involved. I dread falling flat on my face in my white suit of armor. . . . I see my problems in learning stemming from a discontent with reality or inadequacy before its complex nature.

As one reads and listens to the trainees' expressions of feelings and experiences during their training, there is a poignant and perceptive reflection of the supervisor's role. Perhaps here, more than in any didactic description, the true meaning of supervision and its essential qualities come through. There is a need for the learner to receive help, a need engendered by the nature of professional learning and by the fact that the person must function in the helping role before he has gained the necessary competence. The needs and demands of the client must of necessity take preference, but we must postulate a potential within the trainee to handle, with help, the stress created by the discrepancy between where he is professionally and what is demanded of him. The approach first utilized is that of helping the trainee to identify the problems that confront him, what the client's needs are, and how the trainee feels about the client and the situation. The supervisor affirms the constructive and useful parts of the trainee's approach and makes known the what and why of his approach that is inappropriate. The supervisor has responsibility for understanding the trainee's feelings, thus accepting the trainee himself, but not necessarily his professional use of himself in counseling.

When the trainee evidences inability to effect change in his counseling relationship and places his difficulties in his own past experiences, the hope is expressed that the trainee may use the present situation to correct past difficulties. If, after mutual consideration of his current capacities, a lessening of anxiety-producing demands, and an attempt to help the trainee recognize and be responsible for needed changes in his work with clients, there is no shift, personal therapy may be indicated.

Dilemmas in the Personal Encounter of the Supervisor and Trainee

The supervisory task is complicated by the fact that supervisors are fallible human beings, who may find it difficult to achieve the ideal of empathic understanding and unconditional acceptance of the trainee. Clinical skills are important, but it is also necessary for the supervisor to understand the teaching-learning task, and to know how to discern and help the trainee with his learning problems. In addition, he needs extensive knowledge of human growth and development, of personal and interpersonal dynamics, of cultural factors, and of how to set in motion a counseling process. The quality of conceptual thinking is important if he is to help the trainee in the application of the theories and techniques learned and in transfer of knowledge from one situation to another.

The person who plans to work with troubled people needs to develop an identity with the helping role to serve as a model for the trainee. The supervisor needs an identity with the service and the setting in which training occurs, an identity with the therapeutic task, and an identity with the trainee and the teaching task. Capacity to maintain a constructive interpersonal relationship with the trainee to facilitate his learning, and at the same time to criticize, to confront, to give or withhold credit, is essential. Some of the attitudes of the supervisor which retard the trainee's learning process are as follows:

Excessive need to be liked. This, in many ways, is similar to that of the trainee whose responses within the helping situation are determined by his need for love and approval. If a supervisor finds it difficult or impossible to accept a feeling of difference, and to accept the role of authority imposed by his function and his greater skill and knowledge, it will be impossible for him to help the trainee grow and develop. He will be too permissive, nondemanding, and overindulgent. The trainee, sensing the implicit demand of the supervisor for love and reassurance, will resent this as an unfair burden and become inwardly hostile. The implication of the trainee's inadequacy inherent in the failure of the supervisor to confront him validly and put out an expectation that he can meet the demands of the situation increases his hostility. The trainee's conflict between the implicit demand of the supervisor for affection and reassurance and his own need to learn and grow is intensified.

Lack of conceptual skill. The supervisor's inability to discern what elements in the trainee's functioning are creating difficulty in his work with clients robs the trainee of needed help. Growth in skill results when the trainee knows what his lacks are, and when he is confronted with his expression of inappropriate feelings, attitudes, or behavior. This failure on the supervisor's part may be related to his excessive need

54

to be liked, so that the trainee is not held accountable for his functioning.

It may equally result from an inability of the supervisor to think conceptually, so that in a certain sense the trainee is taught by description of the supervisor's way of counseling, rather than by either an inductive or deductive process. If the supervisor tends to equate his adequacy with the trainee's development and success, he will be disappointed as the trainee fails to progress. Anger and resentment will build against the trainee. If, in addition, the supervisor does not recognize, or denies, his anger and resentment against the trainee, he is unable to confront the trainee with an honest evaluation of his work. Conversely, the growth of the trainee is accelerated by an ongoing cooperative evaluative process.

Inability to accept his authority. An additional difficulty that may result from the supervisor's insecurities is failure to help the trainee accept the role of learner. As the supervisor's insecurity becomes intermeshed with the trainee's reluctance to move into the learner's role, the relationship may deteriorate into an informal social one with supervisory conferences a pleasant social interchange. As a result, the supervisor is unable to fulfill his teaching and evaluative functions, and the trainee is again caught in a nongrowth-producing relationship.

Imposing the supervisor's image. The authoritarian approach to supervision may be equally destructive to a trainee's growth. The efforts of the supervisor are directed toward telling the trainee what to do, how to do it, and expecting the trainee to perform as the supervisor might. This wipes out any differences there may be between the two personalities. The trainee is not assisted in finding his own style and approach. He does not learn through his own mistakes or successes, and as a result, little learning is internalized or integrated into the functioning of the trainee.

As one looks at the total learning-teaching situation, it becomes apparent that neither the trainee nor the supervisor has a simple task, and that each must be willing to move into a learning role within his own specific function. The growth of the trainee's therapeutic competence is the final goal of each. One trainee sums up the training experience very aptly:

> So looking back on it, I think that I am exact when I say that the critical incident was not just some little thing that happened between me and one of the clients. Rather, it was a long hammering away at that very defensive, rational, fearful shell I had built around myself, and letting it open, and another part of me come out and support that other one. I started out doing things on an intellectual level, blocking out feelings. I ended up by the year's end knowing what feelings were and not being afraid of them. That's really more important. I guess that's what you could say I did. I went from being afraid of my own feelings to not being afraid of them. But it was a long, hard process. Yet the structure of the whole program was a fundamental part in this profit.

Learning any skill or art—and counseling and teaching are truly both—requires practice, patience, and a willingness to be openly human and fallible. In this task trainee and supervisor move forward together.

3

Supervision Techniques with Excerpts from Supervisory Conferences

Emily H. Mudd

In this chapter excerpts from taped supervisory sessions with three trainees are provided to demonstrate approaches in supervision, especially in dealing with realistic problems in marriage counseling. Dr. Mudd illustrates through her different approaches how each trainee is dealt with in terms of where he stands in reference both to ego strength and to level of competence. Especially notable is Dr. Mudd's gentle but firm prodding backed by an overall mood of supportive encouragement.

Emily H. Mudd, Past President of the American Association of Marriage Counselors, has given significant leadership in developing marriage counseling as a profession and in the training of marriage counselors for several disciplines. As Director of Marriage Council of Philadelphia (1936-67) and as Director of the Division of Family Study in Psychiatry, School of Medicine, University of Pennsylvania (1952-67), she was largely responsible for developing the philosophy for marriage counseling which Dr. Appel articulates in his Foreword. She planned and directed the NIMH pilot project out of which this book was created. Her earlier publications were: The Practice of Marriage Counseling *(Association Press, 1951); co-editor, with Aron Krich,* Man and Wife: A Sourcebook of Family Attitudes, Sexual Behavior, and Marriage Counseling *(W. W. Norton, 1957); senior editor,* Marriage Counseling: A Casebook *(Association Press, 1958); senior author,* Success in Family Living *(Association Press, 1965). She is presently Professor Emeritus of Family Study in Psychiatry, and Consultant in the Behavioral Sciences, Division of Human Reproduction of the Department of Obstretrics and Gynecology, University of Pennsylvania.*

Supervision involves a many-faceted approach to both the counselor and the client. It includes, as the previous chapter points out, identifying the nuclear problem. It also includes a conscious and sensitive attempt on the part of the supervisor to help the counselor utilize the very special attributes which make him what he is.

This chapter focuses primarily on reality issues which the counselor encounters with his client and on some practical techniques which have been found helpful in eliciting information and feelings and in gaining perspective in the client's situation. Excerpts from taped accounts of three supervisory interviews with counselor-trainees of quite different personalities and at varying levels of experience illustrate these issues.

Trainee #1

The first counselor-trainee whom we will discuss is a man who had had a fair amount of clinical counseling experience in addition to his teaching position. However, he sensed the need for intensive supervision. Because of his past experience and because he gave an overall impression of being an easily verbal and well-integrated person, the supervisor dealt with him on a fairly direct and sophisticated level. The quotations demonstrate that this trainee was able to take issue with the supervisor and substantiate his point of view when he felt the need. He was also able to make use of suggestions to amplify his information and understanding of the client's situation.

The client in this case under discussion was pregnant with

a child whose father was not her husband. The supervisor is raising the question of how the counselor needs to move.

S: We know her (Mrs. Grant's) feelings about this baby and her determination to keep it, so with the baby due in November one has to move—how?

C: Well, I would say on the one hand with her you have to move gently, but there is a time element there, too. Of course, between now and November you can still move gently, I think, within that three-month period.

S: One needs to be supportive of her return to the marriage—one needs to help her in her feelings of self-worth and . . .

C: Show a great interest in her as a person.

S: She needs to feel that we respect her and are interested in her in spite of her action, which from her point of view is anti-social and guilt-ridden.

C: I would also think one important thing here is not to focus on the pregnancy, because to do that is to focus on what her husband focused on when he first sent her here. The area of focus has to be a lot broader, has to be her as a person, and the pregnancy is just an immediate problem, and a very real one, but just one of the elements in her total make-up as a person so the focus has to be much broader, otherwise it would just be a tool used by her husband to straighten her out.

S: Perhaps what you are saying is that her relationship to you has something of value to her in itself and it is very important that you are interested in her, not because her husband has asked you to be, but because you believe in her potential as a person and value it. So perhaps the fact that you are a man counselor, if she can win through even in a very tentative way to feel comfortable with you and relate to you, then it may be in the end an asset, because she had a relationship to her husband which was not very satisfactory. She had a very supportive relationship to a man who is now gone, and so here is the opportunity to try to consolidate something of self-worth in relation to the marriage and to these four children in terms of the future. (The client already has a three-year-old daughter and two sons.)

This excerpt raises at least two important points in counseling. The first one deals with the client's feelings of guilt toward an action on her part which she feels is against the accepted community mores. The supervisor is searching to clarify the counselor's feelings about this "anti-social" action. Apparently to this counselor the matter of guilt and bias in this area was not a problem or deterrent in his feelings about the client. However, the supervisor pushes a bit further by raising directly the question of the counselor's relationship to the client and its meaning to both persons. This leads further into more consideration of the sex of the counselor versus the sex of the client, which should be taken into consideration in all counseling situations.

The counselor goes on to indicate his feeling that the husband will have continuing anxiety about the child after birth. The supervisor pushes him as to what direction this anxiety might take and interjects something of her own counseling experience. She also raises the question of how the client might behave in the future.

S: Mr. Grant will, of course, have considerable anxiety about what in the future after the birth of the child?

C: He'll have anxiety over whether it is his child and whether it is going to look like him, I am sure about this.

S: And what about his relation to his wife after the child is born?

C: I don't get the feeling that that is going to be that much of a problem.

S: You don't think he will worry that she will step out again?

C: I don't get the impression that he is really too worried about that. He says this to her, but I think that is just a means to hurt her. I don't get the impression that he is really worried about her.

S: Well, he isn't worried now, because she's pregnant, but my hunch is that this will be something which will come into the picture when she is no longer pregnant. I may be wrong but . . .

C: The question of infidelity is rather casual . . .

S: And his feeling of holding her into line by showing her he is also attractive to other women is in the picture now. What will you do with him, what about his relationship to you?

C; Well, for a while I have got to be once again very

supportive. He is trying very hard to establish himself in my eyes, and I think I've got to be supportive and allow him to do that, and while he is doing that help him to express his feelings. Every time he expresses some emotion, then he immediately backtracks and tries to deny that really he does have any feelings. He associates feelings with weakness, and he is in a very inferior position relative to me now and I think he feels that very much.

S: You are a white professional man, and somehow he has to work out his feelings of equality and mutual respect—don't you think? It is very interesting that this man indicates his lack of basic confidence and his need to impress. Here you have a black college graduate with a wife in a semi-professional job, a black couple who are somewhat atypical and above the level of their families, with a kind of insecurity that comes from being different, being conspicuous.

C: Also, I would say that comes from just being part of the people, too.

S: That is right. And coming to an agency whose staff is predominantly white.

This interchange again moves into the question of how much anxiety an individual can handle and how the counselor may be able to help the client in this respect. The supervisor led into the area of ethical dilemmas and the relationship between a white professional man and a member of a sensitive minority group. This was an important area to call to the attention of the counselor-trainee. This section also points up the importance of the counselor enabling the client to grow in his own self-esteem and become more secure in spite of his personal and community problems.

The final recording of this supervisory session covers the responsibility of the counselor working within environmental time limits, the matter of reasonable goals, and the use of collateral personnel. It also stresses that one can elicit additional information in ways that are not overly traumatic to the client. This transcript illustrates how the supervisor tries to deal with the very natural and real anxiety of the counselor by postponing any immediacy of action on his part, and by suggesting a more oblique approach.

S: Well, I think this is an interesting case. Do you feel sufficiently comfortable with each partner to go on with this case with the time limits put into it by the pregnancy? I hope you can plant enough firm relationship between you and each of them so they will continue in counseling during the readjustment period after the birth of the child. Does this seem a reasonable goal to you?

C: The only thing in this relationship at this point is, and maybe the supervisory conferences will take care of it, that possibly the wife's stability might be precarious.

S: As we said before, if she does have a good obstetrician, you could get permission from her to talk with her obstetrician, and you could talk a bit with her about her health with the first pregnancy and her health following, to find out whether there were any depressive elements. As you know, sometimes a post-partum psychosis occurs. Apparently her depression began well after the birth of the first child, and it might be well to know a little more before we head into this birth.

C: I would say at this point it would be better not to go into it right away, because if I explained why, this would be a threat to her. If I just ask for the information without explaining why, she would be-come very suspicious. So it would be better to wait until she has more confidence in a few weeks, until she feels more at home with me.

S: I would just have this as something in mind to ex-plore during the three months before the hospitaliza-tion.

C: She is sharp enough to worry. I was afraid I was being too heavy-handed, but I didn't want to start ques-tioning her about her emotional stability.

S: Oh no, I wouldn't go into it too directly. I would get her to talk about her first child and her relationship to that child, and ask if it was a pretty comfortable pregnancy and go into it obliquely.

Transcripts from earlier portions of this supervisory inter-view indicated that at appropriate spots the supervisor raised the following questions with the counselor. They are given here in the chronological order in which they were asked. Many of these questions are generic and are applicable as helping techniques for the supervisor under a variety of circumstances.

Was that ever clarified at all?

What do you feel are Mrs. Grant's dynamics in view of her relationship to life and to this marriage?

Do you feel she is beginning to establish any kind of relationship with you—that this experience is meaningful to her—or do you feel she is still under orders from her husband?

Is she afraid that you are going to judge her in the same terms that her husband does?

What do you think of the kind of job she has?

So what is your present goal at this point with Mrs. Grant?

Putting her in contact with her emotions. Now, what do you mean by that? How does a counselor put a client in contact with her emotions? Could you explain that a little bit?

Do you feel that having a man counselor is particularly difficult for Mrs. Grant at this time?

I wonder if this isn't supporting to her also. She wants this baby, this baby typifies something that was very important in her life. Is that correct? Do you see it that way?

What does this man look like?

How long has he had the laboratory job and how long has he had the business? What I am searching for is this man's stability. How related is he to a goal and how much can he stay related?

Trainee #2

The next counselor-trainee was a man of learning in his own professional field, as were many of the NIMH Fellows. This man had had little opportunity for individual or family counseling within his religious setting. The whole concept of one-to-one supervision was new to him and accounted for a degree of his discomfort. For these reasons the supervisor spent considerable time in raising questions concerning the actual give-and-take between counselor and client.

The opening of the supervisory interview was geared to give the supervisor more of a feel of how this beginning counselor conducted himself and how aware he was of his client's feelings. Often a client expresses more through his looks and actions during the interview than he ever does in words. This nonverbal behavior can offer leads and guidelines of great importance to the alert counselor.

S: It would be helpful to me at least to hear something of your interaction with Mr. Brooks and then raise some of the questions which either or both of us may have. How does that seem to you?

C: I would agree with that. I would like to add—I guess about five minutes of the total interview was lost at the beginning because I had a little small talk with him.

S: Sure, how did you feel about the interview in general at this time? How does your client look in interview? Does he sit comfortably in his chair, or is he a very tense person when you talk to him—physically tense?

C: I would say he is physically tense, changes position rather often.

S: Does he smoke?

C: At times he smokes, when he is very nervous. I noticed he was quite nervous at a previous interview and he smoked nervously and just put cigarettes out, playing with them. Now sometimes he does and sometimes he doesn't, and I took it as his being more nervous than usual.

S: And how was he this time?

C: He didn't smoke much this time; if I remember, he smoked a little but he wasn't constantly playing with his cigarettes. And when you get in a touchy area with him he will shift position in his chair, and kind of lean over sometimes and rest his elbows on his knees, and things like this.

S: With all this anxiety, it is quite amazing that he is willing to comply with your request to be taped. I like his remarks that you mentioned in dictation: "Well, it's okay, I'm all right on records, so I probably will be on tape."

The next excerpt of this supervisory interview deals with the activity of the counselor versus that of the client. It is noted that silence in a counseling interview may be a very anxiety-arousing situation *for the counselor.* This is often true whether the counselor is experienced or not.

If one can bear with this silence and wait with the client for what he wants to bring up, sometimes unexpected and important sharing is produced. All too often the counselor's anxiety forces him to introduce a topic which may be quite irrelevant to the immediate feelings of the client. Parenthetically, because of the importance of the supervisory session, when the trainee and the supervisor feel that they have arrived at insights of special importance, the supervisor often neglects to alert the counselor as to when to make constructive use of these insights. Of prime importance at the next counseling interview is where the client is in his feeling and thinking, and not where the supervisor and counselor are. Something very vital to the counselee may have happened between interviews, and the counselee should have opportunity to bring this up immediately at the next interview if he wishes to. Insights from the supervisory session should be held in abeyance by the counselor for use when and if appropriate.

C: May I comment here how he stops? He'll say what he has to say, and then he'll stop, and he won't say any more unless you come out and ask him something.

S: How much chance are you giving him on that basis? I notice on your dictated interview that most paragraphs begin with a question from you. Sometimes with a person who is diffident and withdrawn to the extent that this man seems to be it's very helpful to just wait with him and not get itchy yourself, so to speak, but just give him a chance to see where he would come in if you didn't introduce something new.

C: In some of the interviews there were longer periods where I would just wait and see what would happen.

S: And what would happen?

C: Sometimes he would speak and sometimes he just wouldn't.

S: So do you have a rough idea, did you wait a minute? Sometimes a minute can seem a long time when you're waiting.

C: I don't remember; I think I gave him a little longer pause; I didn't give him as much time as I could have.

S. One can use silence with a client quite dynamically. What are the techniques which one can use when he says what he has to say and then stops? What can you do with that stop, besides jumping into another subject, which I think is what you have done?

C: Yes, I have done that, and you are speaking of silence. You can just be silent and see if he will go on or not.

S: And what else can you do?

C: Instead of going to another subject you can reflect whatever he was saying back, and if he was nervous about it, or if he looks like this was hard for him to talk about, you might reflect and say that.

S: Say the fact that . . .

C: Yes, you find it hard to talk about this, or depending on how you felt and how you thought he felt, you could say: "Would you prefer not to talk about this?"

S: Going back to the subject you just finished, there is something else again that you might do. Do you have any other thoughts?

C: You are quizzing me with the silent bit? No, offhand I don't.

S: Well, sometimes it is interesting to say, "It seems as if you don't have anything that you want to talk about particularly and I'm sitting here wondering what you are thinking." In other words, get yourself into it. Silence often makes the counselor more uncomfortable than the client, and one can share one's own feelings about discomfort and anxiety.

C: This question that you wonder what he is thinking is what you often do with a friend, when you sit in silence.

S: Yes, you often say, "A penny for your thoughts." You might occasionally say that during a counseling interview, but you can say the same thing in a little less colloquial way. For example: "I imagine you are thinking about something and I'm sitting here hesitating to ask a question because I'm really interested in what you are thinking."

C: Um huh, yes, that is good. I hadn't really thought about that.

S: A person like this—the way he talks, he has more facility in expressing his feelings than I thought he would from my impression of the recorded interviews. Maybe we could get back to the recorded interview and find out what happened. I have a hunch that you started another question.

Trainee #3

The third of the counselor-trainees was a man of extreme sensitivity both with regard to himself and to others. He was also a man of few words, with a lifelong pattern of presenting the best side of things in an agreeable manner. He was unaccustomed to standing up to hostility or to expressing his own feelings. In the supervisory hour under discussion the supervisor recognized that the client had activated the counselor's anxieties about his own passivity by her aggressive, manipulating ways. The supervisor's goal was to help the trainee stand up to this client, to develop enough confidence in his own ability to resent being manipulated by her and, by implication, by other similar clients. The counselor-trainee would then, hopefully, be able to break through the client's control of the interview in a constructive way and focus on the client's real problem.

The excerpts from the recording begin after the supervisor and trainee have listened to a portion of the tape in which the client has talked at length in her usual controlling way about other members of her family without getting at her own part in these incidents.

S: Let's stop this recording for a minute and discuss it. It seems to me that you tried to get through to your counselee a couple of times. You asked her how she feels, and this is excellent, and then she gets off on one of her long illustrations and you again tried to interrupt her, didn't you?

C: Yes.

71

S: You tried to get through, and this time do you think you perhaps got caught up a little bit the same way as other times by asking who else her mother did this to?

C: Yes, this is the kind of thing I always seem to get trapped in.

S: You get caught up in the story along with your client, don't you?

C: Yes, I do.

S: And what do you think about that question you put in the second time? What do you think that did to Mrs. Thomas when you asked her, "Does your mother treat other people this way?"

C: Well, I think she had the feeling that her mother was partial, sort of favorably so, more toward her brothers and sisters than toward herself, and so my question was a lead to go on with the story.

S: Well, I think it gave her a wonderful jumping-off place to keep you busy listening another while about another aspect of the story. Now, in getting her to talk about her feelings about her mother, what is your goal in this?

C: Well, it seems to me what we ought to be looking for is for her to see how she tends to expect more of people. In fact, she knows intellectually they can't produce any more than they produce, but she still expects them to.

S: When you say other people, whom do you have in mind?

C: I'm thinking specifically of marriage.

S: Good, that's the point; it is her relationship to her marriage that brings her here, and the difficulties that she has with any kind of communication or sharing anywhere along the line with her husband, her need to make all the decisions, to give him the orders and to make all kinds of plans behind his back, including coming here. He still doesn't know about this?

C: He doesn't, that's right.

S: And she still maintains that if we made any move to be in touch with him, she will discontinue counseling?

C: That's right.

S: Well, do you think we can find any other spot to listen to in this interview? What is she telling you? What is the meaning of this in terms of what she is trying to get through to you about her mother and sister?

C: That she is struggling for independence but she is tired of being pushed around.

S: And you asked her again how old she is and she said she was twenty-three. It seems to me a very healthy thing in terms of her development that she is able to tell her sister off. Now, what did you do with all of this? Can you summarize a little further along in the interview what use you made of this in terms of her present marriage and relationship with her husband?

C: No, this didn't enter into the conversation in that interview at all, anything about her family relationships.

S: Now, you say her family relationships. Do you mean her marriage relations?

C: Her marriage relationships didn't become a part of the discussions in this interview at all. I think I got carried away again, as I so often do, about these stories. She began to branch off and talk about relationships with her sister, and you see she has moved from the one she was talking about to another one, and I think that from that point on, I was pretty much out of it.

S: Did you get more and more out of it as the interview went on?

C: Yes, I think I began to retire as the struggle continued.

S: So as you saw the time going were you thinking what the meaning of all of this is in terms of where she was in her marriage? Did you have this in mind?

C: No, I did not have that. Well, yes, in part I had that in mind. Two reflections I had—how long will it take her to run down, and can we get to something?

S: You have been hoping that for a long time, haven't you?

C: I really didn't know how to end it, because the more and more she became enthusiastic about the stories, the more I retired from it.

S: But I noticed that you used in a very pertinent way some of the techniques that we discussed in our last supervisory conference, where we were trying to say how can we get to interrupt this lady because she never runs down. I notice you are using a more or less Rogerian kind of repeating her words several times, which slowed her down, but not for long.

C: But that's an improvement—that's an improvement, because it did momentarily give her a chance to pause and reflect, and this has been almost completely absent.

S: I still have the feeling that she is talking a little more about her own feelings and her own anger about this, rather than describing her mother and saying how impossible she is, which has been her approach about her husband.

C: Yes, well I thought as I listened and heard this just then, I was feeling a little more of her anger coming through all of this. How much difference it would have made in the interview if I had been able to make use of this!

S: And she has never raised the question of coming or discontinuing counseling has she?

C: She hasn't.

S: So, fortunately for all of this, you still have time to get through to this lady.

C: Well, I have the feeling more and more it is as much a matter of her getting through to me as of my getting through to her.

S: What do you mean by getting through to you? I think she feels she gets through to you in all her stories.

C: I think what I really mean is, becoming able to handle the situation so as to give her some things to hold on to. I could have said, for example: "I think we have about four or six more minutes to go. Now let's stop and look at what has gone on in this session and where you think we have come." And if there were any time left, we could have set some goals to begin to look at, and perhaps we could work on these the next time.

S: I think that is an excellent summary, and I think maybe in the next interview you can think of that maybe fifteen minutes instead of five minutes ahead.

The difference in the way supervision was conducted with these three men of different personality and background experience brings home to us the need for sensitivity, flexibility, and sufficient security on the part of the supervisor to be able to modify his or her use of self as the supervisory situation indicates. The supervisor should realize that the supervisory hour is only one or two hours out of the total training week. His relationship to his trainee is only one aspect, although a more personal one, of the learning experience offered through the peer group (see chapter IV), through counseling with a variety of clients, through psychiatric case conferences and other related seminars. Perhaps most important of all for the trainee is the continuing association with other trainees and staff in the institution in which he is working. All these things together constitute learning through a personal living experience which in turn can be utilized with others.

4

Peer Group Seminars

Hilda M. Goodwin

*In her second chapter Dr. Goodwin discusses the unique opportunity
for peer supervision offered by a case-centered seminar. She makes
clear how individual supervision is reinforced by the work of the
seminar. She demonstrates how the trainee's unique problem in learning emerges and thus throws light on his characteristic ways of relating to others. Of crucial significance is the use of the dynamics
of interaction as experienced by the trainees in the seminar.*

*Dr. Goodwin uses actual quotations taken from tapes of seminar
sessions to document her procedures. Her major emphasis is on the
need to experience feelings rather than simply to talk about them.
She sees the seminar as a good place for such experiencing to take
place, provided that the leader and the group members are not over-
come by the felt need to cover certain formal didactic material,
except when directly related to the topic at hand.*

*After describing the training process in the different phases of the
case-oriented seminar, she points up special problems for the seminar
leader.*

The use of small groups has been an established teaching
method in various disciplines for many years. We have found
that the small group, with its concomitant peer supervision,
affords certain advantages when used in conjunction with
individualized supervision for teaching and training in a
counseling practicum. The problems presented by the members within the small group setting are in reality a mani-

festation of the particular individual's way of handling himself in interpersonal relationships. This same pattern will be equally manifest both within the client-counselor situation and in the individual supervisory relationship. Thus, this training structure offers a twofold opportunity for assisting the trainee with his problems of learning as they are demonstrated both within the group and in individual supervision. The trainee inevitably faces internal challenges and shake-ups in coming to grips with individual supervision. It is equally true that in the small group, where the focus is on his actual current counseling experiences, the trainee will face a different expectation and reaction than is present in the more protected environment of individual supervision.

The group offers the trainee emotional support as he moves through the difficult process of discarding some of his old, familiar ideas and feelings, and in the learning of the new. Within the group setting the trainee discovers shared feelings and experiences which tend to diminish his feelings of insecurity and isolation. As the group climate of trust grows, relationships develop to the stage where being part of the group has considerable significance for the members. There is both encouragement and expectation that each member will share, when appropriate, feelings and experiences as openly and honestly as possible. The peer support afforded in relation to acknowledgment of attitudes and feelings encourages increased self-awareness and acts as a reinforcement of learning. In addition, there is a broadening of individual experience through learning from each other's counseling case presentations and the "feedback" offered by the peer group. This feedback assists the individual trainee to discover and assess more realistically his own strengths and weaknesses in the way he uses himself within the helping relationship.

Philosophy and Focus in Training in the Small Group Setting

We believe that the counselor, if he is to offer a genuine and disciplined concern within the helping relationship, needs to be aware of his own feelings, attitudes, biases, and values as he uses them within the face-to-face relationship. Thus a primary effort is to set up a process which will facilitate the trainee's development of greater self-awareness, and thereby personal growth, as a necessary condition for development of greater professional competence.

Each person in the group brings his own learning pattern —i.e., his way of dealing with his anxieties in a new situation, of attempting to gain acceptance in interpersonal relationships, and of mastering the new situation or experience. Often the major hindrance to the trainee's development of greater flexibility and sensitivity in the helping relationship is his use of automatic and at times inappropriate responses, of which he is not consciously aware. It is therefore important that efforts be made by the training staff, early, to delineate the trainee's characteristic way of relating to others, so that he may be helped to become aware of it and, where necessary, effect change. Small group interaction offers a unique opportunity for the trainee and the training staff to become aware of the individual's particular learning pattern, i.e., his automatic reaction and response in interpersonal relationships.

A secondary emphasis in the group is on acquisition of necessary knowledge concerning human dynamics, cultural factors, and processes and techniques of counseling.

Content and Method

Each trainee is responsible for presenting his active counseling cases to the group. Occasionally, taped material from live interviews is utilized. Presentation of didactic material is kept to a minimum and is related to the needs inherent in the specific case situation under discussion. Assigned reading is geared to specific topics related to the case situations. Centering information and discussion relevant to marital counseling and human behavior around living people and active, ongoing counseling situations furthers the trainees' capacity to integrate new with prior knowledge.

Role-playing by group members is used as a way of actively engaging the trainees in experiencing and responding to spontaneous interaction, such as occurs in counseling.

A psychiatrist, trained in marriage counseling, in separate sessions relates psychiatric knowledge and syndromes to adult marital problems.

The usual factors common to group process are present —cohesion, group norms, cooperative processes, conflict, patterns of interaction and communication. The implications of these for understanding and working within the helping relationship become part of the content; for example conflict, which may generate strong feelings that break through defenses, may be utilized to help the trainees understand more poignantly what the clients feel under stress.

Process as used here refers to the constantly moving and changing interaction of feelings, thoughts, attitudes, and behavior that takes place either within a one-to-one relationship or within a group. The process in the group involves three interlocking circles whereby growth of the self professionally, greater understanding of the helping process, and greater understanding of one's own and the other's behavior interlock and achieve meaning. Each part moves simultaneously, sometimes with one aspect ahead of the other, but with eventual integration of all three, so that these become part of the trainee's immediate living experience. One of the great difficulties in describing group process is the effort to put into words what happens in a moving and living relationship. In the atmosphere of trust which develops, the immediacy of the living experience of each trainee as he reveals his ways of thinking and counseling, as well as his feelings and learning blocks, vivifies his understanding of the growth process and of change within a helping relationship.

The leader is responsible for direction and movement toward the defined goals of the group. He needs to be aware of the feelings he is experiencing and, when appropriate, share these with the group. He also has to be willing to risk moving into direct personal encounters with individual trainees and/or with the total group when indicated.

Process in Beginning Phase

Each person, including the leader, moving into a small group learning situation experiences anxiety. One of the anxiety-provoking questions for the leader is whether or not this group can be moved into a cohesive learning process. Each group develops a distinct personality of its own in terms of the psychodynamics of the members and their inter-actions with each other and the leader. As indicated, the focus throughout training is on offering the trainee an opportunity for a renewed experience of genuine feeling in-volvement with other persons and with himself. If the trainee can permit himself to again become poignantly aware of his genuine feelings, unmasked, he will be able to perceive others' feelings and stresses more clearly. The leader of the group, early in the group sessions, presents an openness to expressions of both positive and negative feeling. The fol-lowing taped excerpts from an evaluative session held near the end of a training year reveal typical reactions ex-perienced by group members to an expression of feeling by the leader. The leader stated: "Beginning with a new group always makes me anxious."

Mr. D: There was something comforting as you told us about your fears, because we were feeling the same way. It was reassuring to know that I was not the only one who was afraid.

Mr. M: Somehow I did not believe that a person in authority could be afraid.

Mr. L: I heard her say it, but I didn't want to believe it. I wanted a leader who was perfect.

Mr. D: I did not want a leader who was perfect. It was the leader's imperfection that was therapeutic.

Mr. L: When we come into a group and feel unsure, we need to believe that the leader is steady and secure.

Mr. D: But that implies that if one is open and honest about his feelings, he is insecure. I think the fact that I can say that I am churning inside represents the kind of security that you are talking about.

Mr. F: Another thing that complicated it for me was that I did not want to be involved. I wanted to be given answers.

As one looks at the reactions experienced, there is fear of difference, distrust of authority, the need for perfection in the leader, and fear of involvement. The procedure does, however, involve the group members in a beginning experiencing of the impact on them from open expression of feeling.

As indicated earlier, it is important to help each trainee become aware of his particular way of relating in the helping relationship. We find that each individual's particular learning problem may be tentatively revealed during the first weeks in the group as the members share with each other their inner images of self as counselors:

Mr. G: I would like to start with my assets. I feel that

I am an accepting, understanding, kind counsel-or. I am willing to listen with empathy to the client, and I try to express hope and optimism about the client's ability to change himself.

Following this description, one of the psychiatric residents remarked quietly, "I hope I will be that good by the end of the year." Others shared as follows:

Mr. H: I struggle with my tendency to want to tell the client what to do. When I catch myself doing this, I become too passive and do nothing. I feel that I have to know the answers or I fail.

Mr. K: I find emotions more difficult to deal with in a counseling interview. I deal with ideas much more easily. I expect to find it more difficult to talk with people out of the context of the ministry to which I have been accustomed. People expect a minister to tell them what is right and wrong.

Mr. Z: I am a person who likes to be loved and approved of by everyone. I have a real struggle with my need for acceptance from the client. My biggest reason for being in the program is to make some connections with why and what I am really like.

Mr. M: I find myself fearful of any human involvement. It is much easier to maintain an external, easy-going attitude than to get involved.

It is interesting that each of these trainees, in giving his own image of himself as a counselor, in reality described what later turned out to be his specific learning problem —i.e., his way of handling himself in interpersonal relationships which creates difficulty or fails to meet the other's need. By and large, these clergy trainees tended to present certain typical patterns: Mr. G., who presents an idealized image of himself which is not connected with his actual performance; Mr. H., who struggles with his need to be authoritative and omniscient; Mr. K., who finds dealing with emotions difficult and feels he must be an authority on right and wrong; Mr. Z., who has great need to be loved and approved indiscriminately by everyone; and Mr. M., who is fearful of any close human involvement.

As the members recognize that expression of feelings and communications within the group are important to acquisition of skill, the group develops a system of mores and sanctions. There is an expectation that each member will share his feelings about the case, the counselor's use of himself, and his reactions, honestly. Anger at a trainee's unwillingness to face his own blocks to learning and inability to face his own negative feelings is expressed forcibly by the group:

Mr. X: Here I tried to do something which is hard for me to do—to express anger—and I get a feeling of complete misunderstanding and rejection.

Mr. Z: I feel precisely the opposite—rejection is coming from the fact that you are denying your true feeling. You put out this martyr business, "I tried and nobody will help me." If you would show openly some of the anger you are feeling at us, you would find a lot more acceptance than you are getting right now. You put on this smiling facade and martyr act and we know it's phony.

As this trainee later stated, "In supervision it is possible to feel that the supervisor does not know or understand, but when ten people tell you that you are wrong, it has a different impact."

For professional persons who have had some recognition and success, moving back into a training situation with peers inevitably creates some special problems. It may be that the role of learner is intellectually accepted, but the person is not yet ready emotionally to give up the accustomed status:

Mr. D: I see myself as a learner. I want to get away from the seminary, where I am regarded as a status person and a leader.

Mr. E: I think you are threatened when you are reduced to a level of equality with the other group members.

Mr. D: But I really am reveling in the role of student. (*Turning to the leader.*) I am expecting to learn a good deal from you this year. I hope you don't mind if I call you by your first name.

Mr. M: (*Responding before the leader has a chance to.*) If I were having lunch with you, Mr. D., I would expect you to call me by my first name, but here I expect you to use my professional title.

It is apparent that Mr. D. evoked considerable anxiety in a fellow trainee, Mr. M., who was fearful of closeness and not ready to relinquish the protection of his professional status. As the group works with a trainee's denial of his feeling of insecurity at finding himself without his professional prop, he becomes able to recognize his problems, and the group members begin to see their status problem more clearly.

Process in the Middle Phase

The members' presentation of their own case material is undoubtedly one of the most rewarding and yet anxiety-producing experiences. As the problems the particular trainee has in relating to the client or in his use of himself as a counselor are worked with, the group members have an opportunity to perceive vividly some of their own problems. These problems viewed externally are less threatening to the trainees' self-images, and therefore each can recognize similar "hang-ups" more easily. Thus, change may be more tolerable and can be integrated. Following are excerpts of a session when the group felt one of the members had evoked overprotectiveness from them in presenting his case because of his inability to handle negativity.

Mr. X: I think we should look at why we have been so easy on A. Why have we been so protective? Are we protecting ourselves?

Mr. M: That might be true, but we also get the message

87

that he wants to be protected. I think this is the chief reason. We are being cued in by the trainee involved.

Mr. N: I think it is just as much our problem as it is A.'s. We can learn from each other's failures if these can be adequately discussed by the group.

Mr. P: I think some of us might be more threatened than others, and I think the group has to be perceptive of this. At the same time, I think there is a need for greater openness.

Mr. X: I think if we start being protective, nothing happens. If we start saying, "We're all different and he can't do it," we play to his weaknesses and defeat him and ourselves.

One of the outstanding factors is the feedback from the peer group. This feedback can be tolerated more easily from the peer group than from the leader or the individual supervisor, and assists the trainee in a more accurate evaluation of his difficulties and competence.

The sessions at times resemble a modified therapy group. They differ from therapy groups chiefly through the group's stated purposes and tasks. We always return to our focus: learning how to understand and counsel helpfully with persons in marital difficulties. The use of live case material as the primary learning device tends to keep the group's concern on the counselor-client interaction. This effectively limits the area of the group's confrontation of any trainee's behavior, feelings, and attitudes.

It is inevitable that there will be personality conflicts

at times between peers. In the following example this struggle becomes clearer to each as the other group members work with what each one is doing with his specific reactions:

Mr. N: I react to Mr. Z.'s aggressiveness because I wish I were more aggressive. Mr. Z. reacts to my passivity because he struggles with this, too, so we set each other off too easily.

Mr. Z: You are right, we both struggle with a tremendous need for acceptance and use "being nice guys" as a way of getting this.

Mr. N: You deny your aggression and behave in an affable manner. You never show your real anger, although your face and neck get red, but you are still "nice." I am learning to express my aggressions, but I fight not to be the "nice guy."

It was apparent that Mr. N.'s expressions of aggression made Mr. Z. uncomfortable, as this tended to cue off his aggressive feeling. Thus, each projected onto the other the unacceptable part of his own feeling and behavior and tried to solve it in the other.

The content of the clients' problems or living situations may present difficulties for certain trainees. As one trainee expressed it:

Some of my blocks to learning have been cultural in nature, i.e., sexuality, Negroes, people who cheat, etc., and are related to attitudes and feelings that have been conditioned by a million messages in my past. While through years of training I have tried to be a compassionate person, the residuals continue to rear their ugly heads from time to time and I am forced to renew the war I have waged since my adolescence.

One trainee in presenting his case indicated that he told his client, who was attempting to talk with him about marital sexual difficulties, that he "did not feel they knew each other well enough to talk about that." Criticism from the other trainees opened the door for considerable discussion of this trainee's and the others' blocked feelings and attitudes concerning sexuality.

In case presentations to the group, the presenting member inevitably reveals his own learning problems. A common problem of the clergy is nonrecognition of their own or their clients' angry feelings or hostility. Mr. J. in presenting his case was very anxious, but maintained a smiling facade which denied any anxiety about his counseling. Part of his learning problem was his great need to behave "nicely" in counseling so that he would be "liked and approved of" by the woman. His problem came to conscious awareness for him in his presentation and the ensuing group discussion. The case is summarized as follows:

Mrs. French is a twenty-year-old, rather pixie-looking girl, whose father died during her childhood. Her mother did not remarry due to Mrs. French's resistance. She died when Mrs. French was eighteen.

Mr. French is a twenty-four-year-old electronics specialist who works at night in order to pursue art work in the daytime. He was an intermediate child, close to his parents, somewhat irresponsible and passive.

Mrs. French complained of unhappiness, that she had lost all trust in her husband, felt he was capable of walking out without paying the rent. He drove her car after having an accident in which his license was revoked. She took away the car keys. He used her paychecks to pay for a stock purchase in which *he* lost money. She took away the mailbox key. She says she has to be realistic to take care of his unrealistic ways.

Mr. French sees his wife as suspicious, accusing him of interest in other women, screaming at him in a high-pitched voice which "shatters" him. She refuses to share his bed or have intimate relations.

As the group worked with Mr. J., he presented Mrs. French as an "immature and mixed-up coed." As the group raised questions about how the counselor saw the interaction in the marriage and each partner, it became obvious that Mr. J. was overidentified with Mrs. French. He resisted hearing the questions concerning Mrs. French's controlling behavior. He defended his point of view of the woman as an "attractive coed." At this point the group pointed out his resistance to "hearing" what the group said and his failure to look at his own overidentifications. This shook Mr. J. enough that he began to recount the demands she had made of him: unscheduled interviews on her terms, her direct physical assaults on Mr. French, and her screaming at him. He began to question why he had been unable to confront her with her hostile behavior and had yielded to her demands for extra interviews. As he worked on this with the group's help, Mr. J. began to recognize his own difficulties in dealing with hostility in women and his need to "placate and please them," which resulted in his meeting his own needs in the counseling situation rather than those of the client.

There are certain phases that a group moves through during training. The beginning, or "honeymoon" stage as the trainees call it, usually continues for six to eight weeks. Through their supervised counseling experience they begin to recognize some of their current difficulties in functioning in therapeutic roles. Beginning awareness of what they need to do to be helpful, but inability to put this into action within the face-to-face counseling situation, creates both anxiety and exasperation. Anxiety (and a minor form of depression) arises when evaluations at mid-term are approaching.

Mid-term evaluations help trainees to get their performance in perspective. A new spurt of hard work and learning begins, as trainees are engrossed with their counseling and eager to work hard in the seminars.

Ending Phase

As the training year draws toward the close, the group begins to feel the shortness of time and "so much still to learn." The group now carries its process with less intervention from the leader, and indicates areas of major concern on which it wants to work. There is a new understanding of the meaning of terms used glibly at the beginning of training. As one trainee put it:

I think communication when it works, as it is set up in this group, is something that is not verbal. It is a series of high or low voltage shocks of recognition. The whole vague morass of words disappears and it's a direct confrontation, whether it is returned anger or returned affection. In this group you somehow confront these things directly as sort of primary emotional experiences. Which means a lot more than words. It's communication with words, but it is something that is evolved—a kind of language of its own.

There is both happiness and a sense of sadness over coming separation from a meaningful experience. Each finds certain aspects of training have had greatest meaning for him:

I am grateful for the fellowship of the group members. Their presence, their comments, and the opportunity to give and take with them in seminars . . . has been one of the vital contributing elements of the year, not only in terms of fellowship but of stimulation, of self-understanding, and of help in counseling.

Another trainee found the meaning of process in growth important:

I sincerely regret that the program is soon to terminate, but I simultaneously have the confidence that the process begun will not terminate with my leaving. The goal I seek requires years—a lifetime—to reach.

Problems of the Group Leader

A leader needs to be flexible, resourceful, and relatively free of undue anxiety. It would be both unreal and untrue to state that it is possible for a group leader to be free from anxieties of many kinds. The anxiety varies with different phases of the program and with different groups. Each group develops its own climate and its own unique relationship to the leader. There is, however, a current myth among many trainees that the leader from the beginning is completely secure and comfortable in the group situation. In reality, the leader is in the middle of a complex of pressures. There is the pressure of developing a cohesive and working group, pressure from the supervisors of the trainees, and pressure from factors in the setting. Often the anxiety of the leader may be triggered by resonance with the anxiety of the group members.

Personalities of group members. The first question is whether a particular group of trainees can be welded into a cohesive, active, working group. Should there be a preponderance of passive personalities, it will be difficult to get active participation going. The same difficulty arises when there are one or more group members with denied hostility, which will have to be confronted and channeled before the group can move constructively. The genesis of these two ways of reacting are somewhat identical, arising out of fears and insecurities. Anxiety is increased and may be converted into anger as the trainee moves into a new and unknown situation.

Group competition. There is always some competition

between group members for leaderships throughout the year, even though it may or may not be recognized as such by the participants. Until the group helps the members involved become aware of their mutual competitive strivings, one-up-manship results rather than productive work.

Conflicts over authority. Unresolved problems about authority and a carry-over of attitudes developed in earlier situations are common, as one trainee indicates:

> I was thinking as I looked at my responses and what I was saying that I was throwing things out for approval and really identifying Dr. G. with my mother, who was domineering. I have been fighting her and against authority all my life. I felt Dr. G. was trying to control me and that she had feelings of animosity against me as an individual. After I talked with her about this, it became clear that this was not the situation.

Training vs. personal therapy. Out of pressing self-need one or more trainees may try to keep the group interaction therapy-focused. This effort may serve several purposes. At times it may be one way of avoiding exposure of counseling skills or lack of them. It is true that the group process has a double focus: getting on with the task and helping the trainee to become aware of and to change feelings and attitudes that hinder constructive use of himself. However, a continuing focus on intrapersonal difficulties of trainees vitiates the purpose of training. Training emphasis is on the professional use of the trainee's self in the interactional relationship between him and the counselee, or between him and his co-workers and peers.

It is interesting that such individuals usually try to convert supervision into individual therapy. They try to keep the focus in supervision on the experiences or traumas of their earlier years, partially to explain their inability to perform more expertly in counseling, but also to divert the supervisor from confronting them with their lacks.

Setting. Part of the pressure on the seminar leader is related to what the trainee and/or the setting can support in terms of working with the negative or hostile aspects of the trainee's use of himself. Often these very areas are the focal point of his difficulties in using himself more effectively in counseling or teaching. It is always a moot question as to how much of the anger or hostility can be brought into focus within the group without creating undue anxiety.

The essential problem with which the trainee struggles is the problem of change, not only change in his outer circumstances but change in his self-organization if he is to fulfill his own goal of developing greater competence and skill in his interpersonal relationships. Thus there is an inner struggle that the trainee must endure and work through. The struggle is not created by the training; it is inherent in the goal he has established for himself. The struggle has to be the trainee's own, and his to pursue for his own purposes. The supervisor and seminar leader may be able to offer understanding and acceptance of him as he struggles, but they cannot take the burden of this from him.

5

Involving the Learner

Herbert G. Zerof

Professional growth calls for more than exposure to new ideas or the acquisition of new tools. It calls for a very real involvement of the learner in the training process. Dr. Zerof writes a subjective account of the factors that influenced his professional development as a marriage counselor and family life educator. Of particular interest is his stress on the need for the counselor both to be supportive and to provide some in-put in the counseling process. As is true of all the trainees, he singles out supervision as the crucial element in his personal growth, using many specific cases as illustration.

Herbert G. Zerof was a Chaplain Supervisor and Associate Director of the School of Pastoral Care, North Carolina Baptist Hospital, Winston-Salem (1960-63). After two clinical years, one as a NIMH Fellow, he stayed on at Marriage Council of Philadelphia, becoming a Supervisor of Counseling and Instructor in Family Study in Psychiatry, School of Medicine, University of Pennsylvania (1965-68). He is currently Director of Community Education, Hahnemann Medical College and Community Mental Health Center, Philadelphia. In this position he demonstrates the philosophy and approach from his own training experience in the training of mental health personnel: clergymen, physicians, social workers, mental health technologists, and policemen.

Typical of the kind of problem facing the clergyman today is the following:

A young, bright, attractive, unmarried eighteen-year-old girl walked into her pastor's office and said, "I just had an abortion." She went on to say she had met a young man in college, when they were both going to Students for a Democratic Society meetings, and they had gone together two years. Recently they had broken up. She did not realize she was pregnant at that time and since has not told her boy friend.

Her family was straitlaced, affluent, successful in the community's eyes, but unaware of the changes going on in her. They could not understand her views on social and political changes, and in fact she and they had argued about this. They certainly would not understand her more liberal views on sex. She could not bring herself to tell them about her pregnancy. Instead, through some friends at school, she had learned of a physician who had liberal views on abortion and had arranged this abortion for herself through him.

She was surprised that she did not feel guilty about having the abortion, but was upset over the fact that her boy friend had broken up with her. She had no one to turn to at this time. She felt cut off from her family. It was not that she was even angry with them. It was more like they were different and lived in different worlds. She no longer felt she had to fight with them, but felt she had to live her own life in the only way she knew. In the summer she was planning to go out to California and help the grape-pickers in their struggle for better wages.

This kind of problem in marriage and family relationships, so common for the clergyman in today's world, reflects the movements going on in society in relation to this one social institution alone. A couple living together outside of marriage because they feel they love each other; changes in attitudes toward sex, pregnancy, and abortion; gaps in communication between parents and children; radically different social and political ideology in families; and increased affluence and urbanization are all part of the picture of change.

The contemporary clergyman is faced with these problems in a new and different way. He is faced with the personal and family pathos that is created. As teacher and counselor, he is called upon to help people deal with the tremendous conflicts in living that they experience and also deal with his own sense of inadequacy in handling such situations.

Seminaries, teachers, denominational leaders, and clergy themselves as a result of these changes in modern society are viewing education for clergy in an entirely different manner. Education must not only involve learning facts and concepts; it must include attitudes toward learning that allow for the active involvement of the learner. The program of training in which I was involved strongly emphasized the trainee's active participation in his own learning. Thus, the learning became partially a self-conscious process as increased self-awareness took place. This chapter is based on reflection upon that learning process, and is an affirmation of the most significant growth-producing experiences that occurred in the learning process for me.

The Counselor as Congruent

There is no factor in counseling over which the counselor has or should have more control than the therapeutic use of himself in the counseling relationship. Recent research has indicated the critical importance of the counselor's personality in counseling. Carl Rogers, for example, has carefully studied through empirical analysis the important qualities in the helping person.[1] He indicates that a helping person is one who experiences "congruence," that is, a close harmony between what he *says* and *feels*. This is no mean task. Learning to counsel is not so much a learning of techniques to be applied as it is a task of resolving the discrepancies between what the counselor verbalizes he should do, what he actually *feels* that he should do, and what he actually *does*. The kind of learning experience which came from supervised marriage counseling was one which began to make me aware of the discrepancies between what I *say* and what I *feel*. I vividly remember an experience which highlighted this incongruity for me.

A middle-aged woman, married unhappily for seven years, whom I had counseled for several months, came in and announced to me at the beginning of the hour, "This is my last time!" The woman had experienced frustration all her life. Rarely receiving the kind of acceptance and understanding from her parents for which she yearned, she adopted the attitude of demanding it. Somehow she hoped her marriage would make up for all her disappointments, disillusionments, and unfulfilled desires. But inevitably, through her manner of demanding, she failed to attain these hopes. Even in counseling she was demanding that her husband change to answer her needs.

[1] Rogers, *On Becoming a Person* (Boston: Houghton Mifflin, 1961), p. 61.

When he wouldn't change as she wished, she was ready to quit. In attempting to deal with the situation, I was frustrated and angry. How could anyone meet these insatiable demands? However, part of my frustration and anger, as I came to recognize, was in the fact that she would not recognize me as a helping person. This I felt no one with any sense could deny!

As frustration was met with frustration, I asked her if she didn't recognize that I was trying to help her. Nothing was further from the truth at that moment. Toward the end of the interview I was able to recognize my own feelings a little better and say to her, "You had pretty much made up your mind before coming in tonight that you weren't going to do anything, and you certainly have frustrated me in trying to help you." The point here is that if I had been able to recognize earlier my need to be a helping person, and had it in control, I could have dealt with her more helpfully in terms of what I was *saying* and *feeling*.

In another situation this particular need was more in control. A young physician, married for a year, decided that he and his wife needed help with their marriage.

Angered and distraught by his wife, who had not provided the kind of nurturing he wanted, he was looking for an easy way out of the marriage. When I was not able to oblige him, he began in a roundabout way to question the value of marriage counseling. In focusing more clearly on what he was really saying, I was able to say to him, "You have the right to choose whether to continue or not." My need to be a helping person was still there, but in control. In this sense I was free to speak in this way to him. If he had walked out or decided not to return, I would have been shaken but I felt I could understand it. There was certainly less disparity between what I was saying and feeling.

The Humanity of the Counselor

Every counselor has his limitations. This does not mean that the counselor is not striving toward acceptance and understanding of the client, or that he is not willing to control his own feelings in the counselor-client relationship, but it does mean that the counselor is human. To be anything else would be devastating to the client. In fact, unless the client is convinced beyond a shadow of doubt that the counselor is *human,* help will not be forthcoming.

Let me explain what I mean by being human. I realize that a number of things are rationalized by saying, "But I'm only human." By the counselor's humanity I do not mean an excuse for irresponsible behavior. Rather, I mean being responsibly human. To be human is to come continually to grips with one's own feelings, conflicts, needs, drives, abilities, limitations, and motivations as they relate to counseling. It establishes understanding of one's self as the *sine qua non* of joining the human race. Further, it means that the counselor has some base for relating to the client. The client's distress usually stems from faulty human relationships. Thus the understanding provided through the humanness of the counselor becomes the bridge by which feeling touches feeling and life is restored for the client. The counselor is able to reach out *knowingly* to the client and share with him a new kind of relationship that breaks down the barriers of separation within himself and with others.

Being responsibly human also suggests that the counselor has no right to look within someone else's life until he has looked within his own and has come to the point where he can use himself in a controlled manner that is helpful to others. It is the counselor saying to the client, "Let me try to understand and facilitate your sharing in a new humanity." If the counselor puts out any "shingle," it should certainly be this: "Welcome to the human race."

If I illustrate this by my own development, some further clarification may be given. Like many other ministers I had developed a somewhat benevolent, all-giving attitude toward humanity. I really can't blame this on the ministry, but it is difficult to be human in the way I was describing earlier and also be a minister. Unfortunately, there is an expectation on the part of many parishioners that their minister be somewhat ethereal, "above it all." It is difficult to believe that he is human like others. Furthermore, even the minister can get caught in this unreal role, which results in considerable frustration for both himself and his parishioners.

Initially in training I thought that understanding and accepting another human being was as easy as falling off a log. It was largely an intellectual exercise. I do not mean that I had no concern for others or was not willing to risk myself with others, but I had done less struggling with it. I believe I had the concept of myself as a somewhat all-wise, truly likable person who was adequate in most situations. I was not willing to entertain for long any doubts about myself as a helping person. This was brought home to me in a first interview with a youthful married woman.

Married somewhat impulsively and pregnant before marriage, she was loaded with guilt and self-depreciation as she talked. She made such remarks as, "I'm a slob," and, "I don't respect myself," and came for counseling to be judged. I obliged her somewhat and told her in essence what she needed was respect for herself, without giving her much of a clue as to how this could be accomplished. I had an uneasy feeling about the interview, and in talking it over with my supervisor began to recognize that I was setting myself above her and *being* her judge. Once I was able to identify what I was doing, I was able to be more helpful to the client.

As is often discussed in our marriage counseling seminars, acceptance involves reaching *across,* not up or down, to someone else in a caring manner. It means that the counselor will allow the client to experience "fear, confusion, pain, pride, anger, hatred, love, courage, or awe," as Rogers states it.[2] The acceptance of these "states of being" are dependent upon the counselor's ability to accept the same in himself. Self-understanding is integral to understanding another. An event in my own growth experience brought this forcibly home to me. I was unwilling to accept the anger in myself directly and to struggle with it in a more realistic fashion.

[2] *Ibid.,* p. 62.

My customary response to something that felt like an attack was a disarming smiling reply. It was important to be "nice" above everything else. However, I became aware of the force of my own anger in an experience in a counseling relationship with a young, fairly successful public relations man.

Married for ten years, the father of three children, one of whom was retarded, this young man was bothered by his wife's sloppy housekeeping and lack of sexual response. In his ever-smiling manner he told how his wife had let him down by not providing the things he wanted. As time went on, he began to feel guilty about his part in the marital difficulties. Still somewhat immune to direct anger, he was blocked in finding his way out of the labyrinth of his problems. Intellectually, I knew this anger was present, but I too was blocked in comprehending its emotional significance. When the full force of my own anger hit me, I could begin to perceive the devastating effect this denial was having in my client's life. I had a new sense of direction with him and was more helpful and understanding.

Change in the client is facilitated through empathic understanding. This means that the counselor must have appreciation for the feelings and conflicts the client is experiencing. It means that the counselor must be in touch with his own emotional life in order to connect with what the client is expressing. Emotion speaks to emotion.

It was in the area of emotional awareness that my greatest learning during training took place. Initially my whole approach to counseling was largely intellectual. But I moved from asking questions in counseling to being more perceptive in feeling and understanding as the impact of my training was assimilated during the year.

The Counselor's Skill in a Helping Relationship

Skill is important in any face-to-face counseling relationship, but is even more important in marriage counseling. In disturbed marriages the counselor is not only dealing with each partner, but is also dealing with the marital interaction. Skill is needed not only in comprehending what each partner has brought to the marriage, but also in seeing how each partner's behavior and expectations contribute to satisfaction or distress in marriage. Comprehension of the client and of his marital relationship comes through the process of the client-counselor relationship. Out of this relationship come help and the possibility of change for the distressed person. Help and change are always limited by the client's willingness to change, his goals and motivations in seeking help, and his capacity to use this kind of help. There is thus a balance in the helping process between the counselor's skill and the client's desire to be helped.

What, then, is involved in the counseling relationship? The counselor brings his knowledge, experience, and skill to his understanding of what is happening in the world of the client. The counseling relationship becomes a microcosm which helps the counselor to understand the client's difficulties in relating and, hopefully, helps create a new kind of relationship for the client—a relationship that can be transferred to others in his world. To the counseling relationship the client brings all his frustrated expectations and hopes, the disillusionment with marriage, and the pain, angers, and distorted attitudes and fears that have resulted.[3] In the counseling relationship the skill of the counselor is revealed in his freedom to see and hear what the client tells in words, tone, and behavior; his ability to draw from professional content and experience the meaning of what he sees and hears; and the capacity to bring these two factors together in his personality so that he may use himself creatively for the client.

Further, the flow of this relationship gives some real indication of what is happening to the client. How the client is defeating himself in the marriage relationship, what distortions he places on the counselor, and how even his earliest family relationships have caused him difficulty are all seen enacted to some extent in the counselor-client relationship. The counselor's understanding of these factors is also a key to knowing how to help the client.

Another clue to understanding what is happening in the counselor-client relationship is the feelings and attitudes of the counselor himself. Properly understood, they can be a clue to the difficulties the client is experiencing and thus a guide to the help needed. In this sense, the counselor lends his ability to perceive reality to the client. Let me illustrate this from my own experience.

[3] Cf. Harry Stack Sullivan, *The Psychiatric Interview* (New York: W. W. Norton, 1954), pp. 25-27, for a discussion of the distortions brought by the client.

The young public relations man referred to earlier had difficulty in perceiving what really happens in some of the situations he faced and had faced. His whole pattern of behavior was somewhat self-defeating. This sense of failure was heightened when the problems of marriage became overwhelming. Learning early to feel guilt over situations where he was actually wronged, he was able to change his way of looking at things in adulthood, especially as it related to marriage. In discussing the earlier situations that began this pattern of behavior, I sought to put in more realistic responses to what actually happened. For instance, when he was expressing guilt over situations where he was actually wronged, I remarked, "It must have really made you angry."

Through responding to him in this way I was hoping to accomplish two things. For one thing, I was trying to help him perceive a new way of looking at his problems that was hopefully more realistic. Second, I was trying to offer some stimulus to help him break through his old pattern of behavior that left him feeling inferior and unable to cope with his own problems, thus opening new ways of handling problems in a more adequate way.

Perlman suggests that all growth-producing relationships contain somewhat opposing elements of acceptance and expectation, support, and stimulation.[4] Expectation and stimulation come within the context of acceptance and support. Expectation means the anticipation that the care that is being

[4] Helen Perlman, *Social Casework* (Chicago: University of Chicago Press, 1957), pp. 67-68.

expressed will result in some responsive behavior. Stimulation refers to the nudge that the counselor gives toward change.

It must be remembered that the counselor's use of himself takes place in the kind of relationship that should allow freedom. That is, both the counselor and client should feel free to respond to each other. To be sure, this freedom will be limited by the degree to which the client feels free to participate in the counseling process. The counselor, however, must be aware of and respect the client's right of choice.

The Importance of Supervision in Learning

Skill is related to how the counselor uses his own attitudes and feelings in the counseling relationship. This implies that the counselor is able to face honestly these feelings and attitudes, and is able to separate out his own distortions from what is real. Supervision at its best provides this. The experience of supervision is rarely pleasant, especially when one's attitudes or behavior interferes with helping the client. The trainee may not want to change or may find it difficult to change. But change is necessary, if the counselor is to take seriously his responsibility to the client.

"Objectivity" must continually be sought after by the counselor. The more he is willing to subject his feelings and attitudes to the scrutiny of another in supervision, the more he will be able to control them in counseling and use himself more helpfully for the client. Such self-learning is a continuing task throughout life. Hopefully, the need for supervision will diminish as the counselor's "objectivity" or self-awareness increases, but there will always be occasions when he is blocked in self-awareness and needs someone else's help in understanding why. The professional person has a continual responsibility to the client in this respect.

In marriage counseling where one counselor is dealing with both clients the need for supervision is even more imperative. Dealing with a complex of attitudes, feelings, interactions, and values, the counselor is more vulnerable to taking sides, overlooking or distorting behavior, and imposing his own values as to the meaning of marriage. Supervision provided for me during the year an opportunity to understand better some of these factors in myself as I was seeking to help clients with their marriage.

Conclusion

The heart of the training experience is the developing awareness of the use of self in counseling and growing control in that use of self. As simple as it sounds, effective use of self in marriage counseling requires a background knowledge of psychodynamics and of social and cultural systems and a grasp of a variety of marital interactions. It necessitates a degree of self-awareness and understanding of the helping relationship. The use of self involves being open to change in oneself as well as a responsible dedication to the task of helping others. These personal resources and understandings do not come readily, nor without frustration. Many times I felt I was losing instead of gaining ground. However, it was through a learning experience which involved full personal participation in action under supervision that new vistas of using myself as a helping person were opened up.

6

Risk and Reward: Learning Through Experience

Edmund V. Glomski

Writing of learning through experience, Father Glomski shares a quite personal account of his reactions to becoming a counselor. He emphasizes the limitations which surround any counseling process. He stresses the responsibility which the learner carries for making use of training opportunities. He deals openly with the risks inherent in growth, but challenges the learner with the expectation of satisfying reward. His use of case material emphasizes the experiential nature of learning.

Edmund V. Glomski is Professor of Moral and Pastoral Theology at Maryknoll Seminary, Maryknoll, New York.

I learn through experience. Knowledge, skill, wisdom cannot become mine through intellectual activity alone. As a professor this has been repeatedly brought to my attention by self-awareness and by those whom I have attempted to teach. What I make my own through a personal living experience I can transmit to others. Ultimately, this is the determinant of those areas in which I am most comfortable with myself, most at ease with the subject, most likely to have mastered the field, most successful in communicating with students.

Time and again students have expressed their reactions

to my attempts to teach "what is in the book" and to teach what is genuinely part of my own self. They are not only keenly sensitive to the difference, but they proclaim loudly that it is the latter to which they respond and from which they learn.

Counseling as Involvement and Responsibility

The man who attempts professional counseling enters into a relationship that is as demanding upon him personally as it is upon the one seeking help. The counselor commits all of himself: his strengths, his weaknesses, his wisdom, his ignorance, his potential, his limitations. He asks the client to take a scrutinizing look both at himself and at what he does, to be open, frank, and honest.

He asks the client to venture into a growing experience that is often unknown, seldom easy, sometimes painful, yet promising in unexpected rewards. The client is suffering from unhappiness in his life situation. The means of help the counselor can offer is the counseling relationship. The process is painful and difficult, but hopefully the pains are growing pains.

The maturation that is asked of the client is not possible unless the counselor himself is willing to become involved. By its very nature the counseling relationship calls for a personal involvement not on the level of knowledge and expertise alone. What is expected of the counselor is that he share himself. And the price that the counselor is asked to pay is high, for some demand is going to be made on his person. This is the risk that each counselor runs when he commits himself to a relationship.

Reality Limitations

As an integral part of any relationship the counselor must learn to recognize reality factors which lie outside himself. The counselor is working with the limitations of nature of service, time, frequency of interviews, etc., that are imposed of necessity either by himself or by the agency with whom he wishes to be identified. He must ask the same thing of himself that he does of his clients: to live realistically within the daily structures imposed by the specific community in which he lives and works. Provided the framework in which he functions is reasonable and realistic, no one need feel guilty for not being able to render some specific assistance that lies beyond the given structure.

The established framework in which anyone functions is one external reality factor. A second is the nature of the demands and personal limitations which the client brings to the relationship. In the case of Mr. and Mrs. Franklin, the husband felt that he could work only with an older counselor who would also be married. The request at first made me anxious because my first reaction was, "What has gone wrong?" When it was placed in proper perspective, I saw it as a reasonable request which the agency could meet.

A third external reality factor remains to be mentioned: What can realistically be expected of the counselor-trainee at his present level of competence? The dynamics of learning require that anxiety be generated by demanding more of the trainee than he can give in view of his past and present competence. The anxiety serves as a stimulus to grow to meet the new challenges he now faces. The degree of anxiety provoked, the amount of expectation he thrusts upon himself or others, however, must not exceed reasonable limits. What can the traffic bear? Otherwise the counselor might panic at his inability to meet these demands, and the anxiety becomes a deterrent rather than a productive stimulus to growth.

The counselor, then, must be aware of what he can reasonably expect of himself and not let his compulsiveness drive him toward the impossible.

Both the counselor and the client must make choices; and the nature of any choice is limitation, the exclusion of other possibilities. The choices which the parties must make will determine the focus of the counseling process and establish whether or not this client and this counselor can reasonably hope to be engaged in the process. Unless this phase is worked through by all concerned, the counseling process will either abort or prove fruitless. The one who wishes to counsel, for instance, cannot assume the role of disciplinarian.

The Counselor's Vulnerability

The demands which the counseling process and the client himself make upon the counselor will inevitably highlight the counselor's weakness. Then anxiety is triggered; the wish is to retreat, to repel, to press the panic button, to sever the relationship as being unreasonable. A lack of sensitivity, a callousness, a stupidity is projected onto others. I remember how easy it was to justify a client's failure to return for counseling as a sign of "her problem." After all, it was Mrs. Franklin who lacked the ability to face reality, to meet the very reasonable and necessary demands I had made upon her! In retrospect, it seems very clear that the problem was mine.

The counselor's greatest asset is his own self and how well he can use himself to establish a relationship. Similarly, his most destructive liabilities are his personal weaknesses, to the extent to which these remain anonymous or ignored and hinder his free use of himself. If the personal problem is something which he has already faced and integrated, what was once a weakness now becomes a source of strength and an asset in empathizing with the client. With Mr. Matthews, I was at a loss to determine precisely what had been his home experience to explain his present rejection of his parents. When Mr. Matthews finally was able to discuss the conflicts he had experienced and how they accounted for his present attitudes, I had quite a few mixed reactions. I identified with Mr. Matthews' emotional experience and understood the impact of what he was relating in the interview. I saw Mr. Matthews as having gone through much of the same struggle that I had experienced. What was important was that I was able to understand and accept Mr. Matthews, at least in part, and to use my own experiences and not become identified with him in an emotional bind.

Various factors accounted for a successful outcome in the interview: the counselor's awareness of his own sensitivity

115

to the subject matter, a personal resolution of his difficulties, an awareness of the reaction that the client's problem in this area could cause in the counselor—all these amounted to the counselor's ability to work with the client in an emotionally volatile area.

If the personal problem has not been integrated, the counseling process can suffer, and probably will. Working with Mrs. Matthews, I had failed to be sensitive to her hostility, and the relationship and productive work were obstructed. Attempts to explore various areas were aborted because I had not dealt with this fundamental emotion.

With Mr. and Mrs. Potter, I became aware of my own anxiety when confronted with hostility and brought this up with the supervisor. Upon discussion, a pattern began to take shape. Having failed to be comfortable with hostility in my own life, having felt a deep personal need to suppress and deny it in myself, I could not easily accept it in others. The clients were subsequently frustrated in their attempts to vent hostility, whether uncalled for or clearly justified. I had to resolve what this implied in myself and my approach to clients. Only then was I able to move ahead to be sensitive to hostility in these and in future clients.

Similar examples could be cited for varieties of emotional blocks that I, as counselor, became painfully aware of and had to learn to deal with: struggles with authority figures, need for self-acceptance, being judgmental. Situationally they all have a common characteristic in that their presence and effect were highlighted in the process of learning to be a counselor.

Possibility for Growth

Since the most vital factor the counselor brings to the relationship is himself, he must be intimately familiar with his strengths and limitations. To achieve this, the first and most fundamental quality that is called for is the willingness to learn. The learning experience into which he ventures is a journey ridden with anxiety from the emotional impact of the material with which he works. The tendency is always there to relax, to withdraw into former patterns of behavior, to seduce one's self into complacency with a limited self-awareness. This perhaps is the very first tentative insight that the counselor must attain: an awareness of just how willing he is to grow. A conflict that causes anxiety, an expectation made by the supervisor, a realization of how inadequate he is, a confrontation with his self-deception, a realization of how restricted his concept of counseling is, an awareness of the fact that he does feel threatened—some such crisis is necessary to test and to prove that he is in reality willing. The trainee says, "Yes, I want to be here." But then he is told, "Prove it!" When the trainee begins to get some awareness of the price that he must pay, then he is ready to evaluate his desire to learn.

The trainee must also assume the primary responsibility for his professional development. He must stop asking the supervisor, "Tell me what to do; show me where I'm wrong." The counselor must see through his own denial and projection and say, "This is my life, my responsibility." It is at this critical stage that he discovers whether or not he really has the will to learn.

What one looks for in the trainee, then, is a security that potentially will express itself productively in a two-fold manner. It will enable him to look at himself frankly, not to be thrown into a panic by what he sees, and to be keenly aware of what he does see. Second, it will enable him to focus on the client and respond to his needs as he unconsciously uses himself.

Stated differently, the counselor must possess the capacity to live. He must be sensitive to life experiences, first in himself. It cannot be the sensitivity of an open wound, but that of a poet. The former causes the sufferer to be pre-occupied with protecting himself, to center on himself and his feelings, to withdraw from contact with others. The counselor is keenly perceptive of the feelings of the other whom he must try to accept unconditionally, and by whom he is in no way threatened.

I feel that if there is one truth which I have grasped from my training experience it is this: the most vital factor I can bring to the counseling relationship is myself. As a corollary, I would add that my effectiveness as a counselor is gauged by the degree of self-awareness I have achieved.

7

Supervision in Family Life Education: Experiences with Black Mothers and Delinquent Girls

Sylvia R. Sacks

In two illustrative case studies Mrs. Sacks points up the crucial role of supervision in family life education. In particular she stresses extensive preliminary preparation, close contact during the field assignment, and attention to the trainee's basic problems.

In her concept of the counselor-educator role, Mrs. Sacks adds a new, thought-provoking dimension to the pastoral counseling task. Her stress on acquaintance with and understanding of subculture is noteworthy. By expanding "sex education" to include attitudes about interpersonal relationships at large, she suggests a whole new area of interest for clergymen, an area particularly relevant for the needs of the day.

Sylvia R. Sacks was Chief Supervisor of Family Life Education, Marriage Council of Philadelphia (1961-69) and Consultant (1969-70). She was Instructor in Family Study in Psychiatry, School of Medicine, University of Pennsylvania (1959-67).

In our contemporary world, the breaks with tradition have been romanticized by folk-rock ballads and flower people. In our universities, students are propelling themselves into participation in decision-making roles. Our fears of family disruption are being substantiated by divorce statistics and war. These dramatic changes are bringing an increased number of requests to seminaries and universities for professionally trained family life educators.

To meet these educational needs during this period of cultural and economic transition, church and secular leaders are conferring about courtship, marriage, and family life challenges. Even as they organize educational courses for teachers, there is continuing debate about values, content, leadership roles, and trainee involvement and responsibility. Some leaders stress, as Pope Paul recently indicated, "a great need to restore the sense of sin to the conscience of man." Simultaneously, others seek a less traditional door to enter into modern man's consciousness.

Family life education training follows a counselor-educator approach, wherein the feelings in human relationships are woven into the facts of human existence. More specifically, our goal is to sensitize educators and to deepen their understanding of marriage and love relationships, while developing new teaching skills.

The Scope of the Program

In the family life education sequence each trainee participates in a minimum of six leadership experiences. Assignments are in group leadership, with other trainees serving as observers evaluating their colleagues. In the experience out of which the findings in this chapter were drawn, the family life education seminar was led by the author of this chapter and was designed for pastoral educators who would prepare parish clergy to lead youth and adults in discussions of man-woman and family relationships.

In our work with pastoral educators we do not enter into theological debate; rather, our mutual focus is on man's relationships to man. We see our task as the presentation of a particular educational model. We provide such an experience in order to give each trainee an opportunity to evaluate this educational model for his own teaching.

Philosophy and Educational Goals

The philosophy of the counselor-educator model of family life education employs an approach that seeks to offer new knowledge to people. A second and concurrent goal is to develop a leader's perceptiveness about men and women's feelings in their varied dating, courtship, engagement, marriage, and family relationships. As the leader's perceptiveness is expressed and felt, an audience often becomes more emotionally involved, more sharing, and thus more available for attitudinal change and new learning.[1]

Teacher preparation for such a process emphasizes the development of (a) the teacher's awareness of his own defenses, attitudes, and values—e.g., "Prior to this series I had denied the physical in man-woman relationships"; (b) the teacher's capacity to reach for the personal and deeper feelings which underlie many of the audience's glib answers about affectional attitudes in dating, mating, and family living—e.g., how to respond when a boy exclaims, "It's better to love 'em and leave 'em!"; (c) the teacher's ability to offer skills for increasing competence in human relation-

[1] Sylvia R. Sacks, "Marital Interaction: Insight for Physicians' Roles in Sex Education," *Pediatric Clinics of North America*, XVI (May, 1969), 459-70.

ships, at any age or level of affectional behavior—e.g., the skills needed to keep each other close, to give and to receive affectional responses. We believe that if men and women can become more sensitive to each other, they will find a way through "the lonely crowd" to continue near each other in more sustained relationships.

Many new questions arise when a counseling philosophy that grows from listening to men and women first, to understanding what pleases, hurts, encourages them personally, comes in contact with an educational stance that is supposed to know and give right answers. What happens when preaching and teaching add listening? Can we teach teachers through educative group techniques to be more perceptive of human emotions? We are aware that the traditional educator has often taught his deeply studied answers authoritatively. Can he now encourage persons of the audience to enter into a dialogue, to question or to disagree? We are also aware that the traditional clerical appeal has generally been to higher reason and deeper faith. Can clerical leaders encourage participants to express feelings and deep emotions —anger as well as affection, dejection as well as joy? We know of the dependence of educators upon planned agenda and formal curriculum. Can they now allow youth or adults to loosen such a format? Can the teacher be asked to teach, yet to hear and to listen, too? We believe that the interdisciplinary approaches of counseling and educating can be tied creatively to new leadership roles. Our goals to integrate philosophies and methods further have been tested in varied field experiences.

The educational model for training in family life education seminar. In our experience, each year's training group meets for a weekly seminar. Topical discussions range from values and life styles of poverty and blue-collar families, to the social-sexual problems of young and old in a variety of economic brackets.

Community practicum. Leader-trainees help to plan and lead family life education meetings, usually a series of four to six sessions. These might take the trainees to an affluent, tree-shaded suburb or to a ghetto-blighted neighborhood. Radio, TV, and community conferences have been a part of some field assignments.

Supervision. Each leader-trainee is individually supervised. An important area of supervision is his understanding of the people he will be working with. His personal attitudes on masculine-feminine roles, on courtship and marriage, on the use of the pill, on permissive sex play are discussed, along with the effectiveness of his preparation for the meetings. His interactions with his assigned group are reviewed from tapes of his meetings.

Reports. Some written assignments help trainees reflect on their personal attitudes in sensitive areas; e.g., write out your reply to young people's question: "What should we do about premarital sexual desires if we are going steady but cannot plan for marriage for a number of years?"

Written evaluations are collected to provide a three-way perception of the field experience.[2] Included are:

[2] Sample forms and other materials in a "Family Life Education Kit" are available at cost from Division of Family Study, University of Pennsylvania, 4025 Chestnut St., Philadelphia 19104.

a self-analysis evaluation from each leader-trainee;

an evaluation form filled out by each participating group member;

an evaluation filled out by a colleague assigned as observer-evaluator.

Counselor-Educator Learning Experiences

In our own experience, we have begun with a discomforting assignment. Each leader-trainee was sent to a group that was not of his faith (e.g., an Episcopal minister was assigned to lead sixteen-year-old boys in a Roman Catholic high school; a Protestant professor led a Jewish single women's group). Since the counselor-educator approach suggests involving persons emotionally in order to form new attitudes, each leader's change began by his involvement in an unfamiliar but guided experience. In addition, no man was to wear his collar or church garb on his assignment. No pulpit would be used, no homiletic reference or biblical text would begin a meeting. To his group, each was designated as a "special lecturer" from the University of Pennsylvania's Division of Family Study.

Despite some uncomfortable hours, many trainees later reported that this beginning did indeed lead to a reappraisal of leadership habits. Stripped of familiar methods and ecclesiastical supports, each man had to begin to work through to a new self-concept in his leadership. One professor put it this way: "I felt as if I were asked to build a church with one hand tied behind me." The dynamics of this integration

124

may be better seen through two actual learning experiences wherein the trainees changed their leadership approaches. The first example is with a group of mothers of teen-agers in a substandard, primarily black neighborhood. The second example is of a leader with a group of juvenile delinquent girls.

Example 1: A Black Mothers' Group

The leader-trainee, Dr. Parker, was a professor of pastoral care and psychology. His goal at divinity school was to teach younger clergy to lead family life meetings. His field assignment here was in a Methodist church in a gang-run, alley-lined neighborhood. He was to meet with the parents while other staff met with the teen-age boys and girls.

He reviewed his plans with his supervisor. He would go first to the church and attend a Sunday worship service. In the process of supervision, he began to realize that he needed rather to hear and see where the parents and children lived, to be in touch with the troubled moods, the restlessness on street corners, and the concerns of a girl, boy, or parent living there.

For his series of six meetings Dr. Parker used two films: one on a boy's bodily changes in growing up; one about a girl deserted by her boy friend after being infected with VD from him. After the first two meetings Dr. Parker lost his professorial cool! His audience seemed disinterested and less talkative than he had hoped. Questions were not about the film facts but about personal dilemmas— how to keep a girl off the streets or a son out of a gang.

In supervision we replayed the taped meetings. The women's comments after the VD film were, "That's the way a boy will do. . . . What else can you expect from boys or men?" Dr. Parker had turned the discussion back to public health facts, not utilizing the openings given by the group. Facts had been presented, feelings had been ignored.

This learned educator had prepared for the meetings by studying sexual facts. He had seen where the group members lived and had reviewed in seminars the life style of the ghetto. But he had yet to perceive what social-sexual relationships meant to these women, where they really lived, and what feelings they were suggesting by their offhand comments. What were they really saying about their expectations of men caring, of being responsible in affectional relationships? Dr. Parker perceived that they often felt abandoned, that they were angry with men, particularly with men's negligence and lack of responsibility toward the family.

In the supervisory session we suggested that Dr. Parker articulate for the women their feelings of anger toward men. Talking about personal hostility between man and woman was a new experience for this teacher; his usual practice was to emphasize the universal aspects of man's love.

To help in the articulation of feelings, Dr. Parker replayed their taped comments to the group. After he shared his understanding of their anger, a completely new discussion began! Now the women talked about "how men made me mad with them," especially "when they depend on you to train their boys." They admitted, "If I am angry, I may not make my son's bed for a week." As feelings drained off in this group of black mothers, some verbalized their need for a man as father, husband, and son. The family life leader then helped the women to see their men as "angry nomads, too, who felt the dice loaded against them." Together the group and leader discussed how women might take some responsibility for including men in more than physical closeness.

The human levels of interpersonal competence were explored. With native humor and wisdom, the women talked together of how to invite men back into their homes and family experiences. With his supervisor Dr. Parker analyzed how he could help them to a new perception of each other's real feelings, how this might nurture new skills and a new valuing of one's self near another human being, and in each partner a new belief in a human relationship.

Some women after the meeting mentioned special personal concerns. Others asked, "What can I do to help a son or daughter to get through high school without becoming an out-of-wedlock parent?" From supervisory discussion, Dr. Parker found he could be of further help by a referral to an appropriate community resource. In evaluating the meetings many participants asked for a follow-up series, commenting, "It's time to quit and it seems like we were just getting started. We need all the help we can get."

In Dr. Parker's written evaluation of his leadership experiences he commented: "This was one of the most meaningful religious and educational experiences of my life. Too much is done in armchairs that never touches the heart of people. No wonder they have no spiritual stomach for programs. In a family life educational approach, I found a way to be effective with people. As I learned to identify and to admit their angers, their hurts, and their hopes, they were ready to get involved in the family's real problems and directions. . . . This educational model offers educators the opportunity to learn how to work with people on the level of feelings and to teach their students this art."

Example 2: A Group of Delinquent Girls

This leader-trainee, Dr. Turner, was a professor of pastoral psychology and counseling. In addition to teaching and writing, he had prior clinical experience in a state mental hospital. His field assignment was to give a sex education course to a group of teen-age girls in the House of Detention, a facility of Philadelphia County's Juvenile Court. Each girl was awaiting trial or adjudication. We had been invited by court authorities to try to influence these girls' attitudes and decisions for future dating and mating. They were already immersed in sexual and moral problems, and had heightened tensions in their relationships to authority figures. Could Dr. Turner effectively enlarge their views of man-woman relations to include the more profound sexuality that considers human needs to keep an affectional relationship alive, with or without the sex act? [3]

Prior to meeting his group, each leader had to assess his own sensitivity to discussing premarital sexual behavior in a written personal reaction report. The report could not be couched in theological terms, as youthful audiences made little connection to biblical quotes, often commenting, "So what else is new, man?" Dr. Turner wrote, "I had to be ready to state my position on premarital sex, infidelity, masturbation, and homosexuality." An important thing was that young people would hear a sincere adult who believed in what he said, and who could convey it in his own words. Not only the leader's views but his capacity to allow for views from his audience was stressed as necessary for a meaningful dialogue. A planning period implemented the assignment, with supervision considered of great importance by this trainee. Dr. Turner reported twenty-two collateral consultations for this series of five meetings!

In supervision we talked of including, early, some understanding of each girl's widened concern: how to find and recognize love and how to be loved in return. First a leader would have to anticipate the girlish dream; then he would need to look at the harsh realities of each one's

[3] Sylvia R. Sacks, "Pastoral Educators Prepare to Lead Youth: The New Sexuality," *American Journal of Orthopsychiatry*, XL (April, 1970), 493-502.

stumbling search in her day-to-day living. The leader could not simply demonstrate his prior experiences and knowledgeability; his content had to hold meaning for these girls—his group—beginning where they were in feeling and in living. Dr. Turner perceived that the locked House of Detention was no bar to a young girl's hopes, but perhaps actually helped her face discouraging days. How would he reinforce the hope, yet offer skills for everyday feminine roles to which many of the group would return? Supervision had tried to guide an educator's considerations away from a now-listen-to-me to an understanding approach.

Dr. Turner's sensitivities grew for his group's past, present, and possibly future life circumstances as he reviewed a filmed television report depicting a Philadelphia depressed area, the gangs who ruled the trash-lined back streets and deserted houses, and a woman who had been raped. He attended as an observer a series on sex education in a ghetto church, led by a colleague. He expressed surprise at the police guard in the church doorway. He wrote: "With supervision, I had been compelled to take a long second look. I began to be aware of the specific cultural coloring to the lives of these girls."

Supervisor and trainee shared in a preseries visit to the House of Detention. We saw a turn-of-the-century building. As guards locked each door and gate behind us, we saw teen-age girls in prison-grey shapeless shifts. They led aimless days—no school classes, no literature, no recreation except for stories from the adult prostitutes. We learned that several teen-agers were already pregnant. What did sexuality mean to them? Had introduction to the sex act been from rapacious slum males or from the sexual attacks of aggressive homosexual female inmates? Dr. Turner grew more thoughtful about what sex education he would bring to these girls. His tapes and written evaluations note what happened in his efforts.

With Dr. Turner at his first meeting with the girls were his supervisor and another trainee, a Catholic priest, professor of moral theology. Fifteen girls, age thirteen to eighteen, had been officially ordered to attend; thirteen came, sitting in sullen silence. Dr. Turner sorted his papers, took out a tape recorder, and with much inner personal anxiety, yet outward calm, quietly asked each girl her first name—and remembered it. He expressed a polite and pleasantly informal greeting to the white, black, and Puerto Rican members of the group. He knew each was uninformed about the series, and he explained it.

Dr. Turner then informally took out a current issue of *Life* magazine with a full-page advertisement of a new car and a young boy and girl in bathing attire near it. Rather than begin with lecture or anecdote, he had decided on this attractive illustration. He added, "My wife and daughter suggested you might be interested in this picture." His very human inclusion of them in his family cut across several shadows. By his approach he had reached them where they were and where they hoped to be. They moved in closer to look and began to react to Dr. Turner's tentative questions about what each saw in the picture, posed in Madison Avenue's typical style to sell cars by using sex appeal!

Emotional and educational involvement occurred for each girl because the situation was nonthreatening, the questions were indirect, and each teen-ager could comment on the opening Dr. Turner offered. Neither preaching nor didactic lecture could have achieved this disarming beginning. In using his insights as a father and a man, the person in the scholar leader came through. After active discussion Dr. Turner, not realizing the full extent of his emotional contact, reverted to his educator's habit of presenting his other carefully prepared data.

In the supervisory session after the meeting we discussed how Dr. Turner might have continued the girls' initial involvement. The couple in the picture had been in bathing suits, the girl in a bikini. Perhaps asking for the group's conjectures about the girl would have sparked discussion of personal physical images that girls carry, or allowed for their projections about themselves near a boy, or perhaps allowed for Dr. Turner's value statement about what qualities other than physical a man might seek in his relationships with a woman.[4]

In the series factual data were also important. Dr. Turner exploded myths about menstrual hygiene, fears about childbirth, and discussed their inquiries about man's sexual responses. These girls were sexually experienced with boys and men, but were seen as misinformed about male and female physical and emotional interrelationships.

[4] Cf. Sylvia R. Sacks, "Widening the Perspective on Adolescent Sex Problems," *Adolescence*, I (Spring, 1966) , 79-90.

Since one of the leadership goals was to enlarge youth's understanding and skills for interpersonal relationships, Dr. Turner in later meetings used role-playing about a just-married couple, home from a Mexican honeymoon. The girls played their roles with lively interest and banter. Dr. Turner asked about how a bride might feel if her new husband did not come home for lunch the first day. The girls realistically said that there was "no use expecting a workingman home for lunch," but talked rather about planning the first dinner. When we later listened to the tape, we heard one of the girls mention that she would prepare "a big pot of beans for the first supper." Dr. Turner commented that he had privately thought in terms of something more delectable. Though inwardly surprised, he allowed them to discuss their first meal as they saw it. He had learned to listen to them, to hold back, and to let their ways of relating in their own life styles come through to him.

In supervision we talked of ways Dr. Turner might have developed this situation in further depth. He might have inquired how a young bride would feel or what she might say or do if her young man came home in a seemingly angry mood. The dialogue between leader and group needs to explore this kind of knotty interpersonal problem. For any couple it is necessary to learn how to argue, to understand what crying, nagging, or the "silent treatment" really suggests, and to recognize how and when to be more open with each other, so they can resolve a problem. Dr. Turner was himself steeped in the kind of religious background which denied or suppressed expression of angry feelings. He had to rethink how anger as well as tenderness can be a wholesome part of love's growth and how these ideas could be woven into subsequent meetings. Later, the girls wrote, "Talk more about the pleased wife, the handicapped wife, the alcoholic wife." They, too, were now stimulated to seek new information and new understanding of how to deal with the mood and behavior of a woman and her mate.

As the series concluded, the girls had known in the leader a compassionate man, with whom they sensed a new freedom to disagree, to inquire, to really talk. Maybe they never understood all of Dr. Turner's words (his trainee colleague observed, "He sometimes talked over their heads"), but from the evaluative materials collected we knew that each girl had felt a new significance as part of a group whose leader was understanding of her. They asked for an extra meeting, which Dr. Turner held. The uses of the counselor-educator approach were further illustrated when four of the girls asked to see Dr. Turner individually for a counseling hour. This counseling function is an important phase of the educator's role, and Dr. Turner arranged for it.

Dr. Turner prepared a postseries report for his meeting with court authorities. Form could now be extracted from function as, from combined experiences, we summarized the guidelines. The counselor-educator approach had involved:

assessing oneself,
anticipating the audience,

articulating content relevant to the
  lives of group members,
acknowledging critical questions and
  evaluative data from the group,
affirming values that enhance man's
  dignity in affectional relationships and for his long-range visions,
availability for brief counseling and,
  if necessary, referral.

Dr. Turner's summary of his personal and professional observations of the learning process mentions the new and difficult experience of being "observed critically." Yet, in retrospect, the immediate feedback from supervision, tapes, and audience had been more "realistic and valuable than any reference bibliography." The teen-age series had indeed abruptly jostled his search of new approaches. Other trainees, after their field experiences, also underscored Dr. Turner's reflections. Each found fresh impetus to balancing a new religious dogma, a structured educational curriculum, and the unstructured outlines of human relationships between man and woman.

Informal Program Assessment

The future potential of this program may be seen at college, community, and national levels. Newly devised teacher training curricula and workshops have already been instituted in several of the seminary and community settings represented by our own trainees. Several men have accepted

135

appointments in Mental Health Centers directing community educational programs for local clergy and others. Eighteen men became consultants to the United States Air Force in chaplain training programs, each spending one month overseas to bring new approaches to military personnel.[5]

Theological leaders are on the way toward taking special responsibility to understand more about man's emotions and to work with man's reactions in his relationships and his life styles. Hopefully, the approach to additional supervised training for teachers, as outlined in this chapter, may help seminary and church become more relevant and their leaders more effective.

[5] See p. 183 below.

8

Meeting the Needs of a New Generation of Theological Students

Robert C. Leslie

Just as Dr. Goodwin sees the peer group as an opportunity for group supervision (chapter IV), so Dr. Leslie sees the small interacting group as a particularly potent medium for learning. He notes how essential it is for the leader-supervisor to be emotionally involved himself if he expects real involvement from the student-trainee. He demonstrates how the "learning through doing" orientation of small groups helps to meet the needs of the new breed of theological students. Dr. Leslie's training as a NIMH Fellow reinforced his conviction that for real learning to take place, both learner and teacher need to be deeply involved. He uses student evaluations to demonstrate the effectiveness of involvement in the group process, and shows how theological doctrines such as grace and crucifixion can be experienced in the group. An excerpt from a taped session demonstrates his counselor-educator approach in working with groups.

Robert C. Leslie has been involved in clinical work with theological students for over twenty years. His interest in small groups began as a Methodist pastor, was furthered in mental hospital chaplaincies, and continues in seminary. He is the author of Jesus and Logotherapy *(Abingdon Press, 1965) and* Man's Search for a Meaningful Faith *(Graded Press, 1967). He is Professor of Pastoral Psychology and Counseling at Pacific School of Religion and the Graduate Theological Union, in Berkeley, California.*

The word that best characterizes the seminary student today is *involvement*. Today's seminarian wants to be involved in direct confrontation with the culture. He wants to be involved in action projects in the ghetto, in political strategy in the city, in power pressures in the suburbs. Moreover, he wants to be involved in educational policy and decision-making on his campus. He wants to serve on faculty committees, determine curricula requirements, and have a voice in faculty tenure. He wants, also, to be involved at a deeper level with people. He wants to live in close proximity to the people he is ministering to. He wants to know his faculty and his fellow students.

One astute observer describes the type of seminary student found on campuses today. These particular students happen to be in a theological school in Berkeley, but they are typical of many students anywhere.

> They tend to be future-tilted, identity-loose, generation-gapped, history-rejecting, power-conscious. What matters to them about Cal-Berkeley is not its magnificent library so much as its student radicalism. They are shaggy and corrosive, impatient with formal education, deeply committed to action as a method of discovery, disenchanted with Systems and Establishments, distrustful of cerebral theologizing, and unconvinced by the church's traditional claims to ultimacy and authority. They want to know, but they want to find out for themselves.[1]

The Experiential Approach

It is very clear that these students are a new breed. In

[1] Wayne Rood, Pacific School of Religion, in an introduction to an unpublished evaluation report of the American Association of Theological Schools, 1968.

contrast to students of ten years ago, who seemed concerned about very little except theology and who appeared quite content to ignore problems of the social scene, the students of today insist on seeing theology and life related, and demand an experiential approach to the pressing issues of our culture. Traditional patterns of education are strongly resisted in a widespread movement toward involvement and participation. Knowledge is sought after, but knowledge that is discovered through personal, self-directed search. It is this quality of self-direction, of finding out for themselves, that is of particular interest to us as we consider a teaching-learning process in a seminary setting. As has been amply illustrated in the pages of this book, the teaching-learning process described here is one in which the students are given opportunity to grow through actual personal experience, through finding out *for themselves*.

As students try to put into words the emphases which are important to them, the distinctions they make are between the "existentialist" and the "essentialist" points of view. The existentialist sees all learning as related to personal involvement in the subject matter. In this approach the attention is put on man as man, and the process is seen as an effort "to give rational form to a vision that must be, finally, intensely personal." [2] One student writes of the need for the kind of education which is "out to . . . minimize peripheral knowledge and to maximize the kind of learning that can bring about a developmental change in personality structure."

[2] Warren Bryan Martin, *Alternative to Irrelevance* (Nashville: Abingdon Press, 1968), p. 49.

In contrast to the existentialist point of view is that of the essentialist, in which the concern is "for that which goes beyond time and place—for that which is permanent, uniform, rational, sure" and which stresses "a specific body of knowledge to be taught and learned." [3] The essentialist thus places a high priority on formal content presentation, often with little attention to the learner as a person. This obviously is the classical approach in education in which the lecture method is the primary means of communication. For the teaching of counseling and of family life education, this method has proved to be notably ineffective.

When students criticize current seminary teaching, their sharpest critique is directed against those courses in which there is little sense of personal involvement. One group of students, in writing about their ideas for the seminary of the future, begin with these words:

> The seminary center will provide opportunities for the members of the seminary to engage in conversation about their experiences and their understanding of it. These opportunities will be designed to draw out people's abilities to explore the ultimate dimensions of their existential concerns, by engaging in theological dialogue with the other members of the community.

These students are asking that their education use their own experience as a point of departure, drawing theological implications out of experiences they have already had. In

[3] Ibid., pp. 49, 52,

another rather similar document a group of students made the following suggestions:

> Wherever possible and appropriate, courses should be problem-oriented. . . .
> Wherever possible and appropriate, tutorial and preceptorial instruction should complement lecture instruction. . . .
> Wherever possible and appropriate, small student-centered, nondirective groups should complement professor-centered and directed groups.

The degree to which the teaching-learning process described in this book meets these suggestions is quite amazing.

Participation in an Interpersonal Relationship Group

I would like to describe a teaching-learning process which has many of the same features of the training procedures described in earlier chapters in this book but which follows a somewhat different pattern. It takes place in a seminary class called "Interpersonal Relationships," a group experience limited to ten students in which interaction among the members and with the leader is the chief focus, a class which capitalizes on the here-and-now, and one which draws its agenda out of the action happening at the moment in the group. Although cognitive content about group process is provided, the learning is achieved far more through being a participant in the group than through studying about groups.

For a number of years I have conducted classes in interpersonal relationships, but it is only since being involved as a student in the training process described earlier in this book that I have sensed the real potential for learning which is present in these classes. Whereas I had previously perceived the class as solely an experience in interpersonal interaction, I now sense that it can be a vehicle for cognitive learning not only about group process but about theological concepts as well. It was the effectiveness of the experience-oriented seminar in contrast to the ineffectiveness of the occasional formal lectures which helped me to recognize the potential of the interpersonal relationship class approach.

Leadership in the Interpersonal Relationship Group

Although it is not my purpose here to deal in detail with the structure of the interpersonal relationship class,[4] a few words are in order about leadership. My task as leader is to try to create a climate of trust in which group members will feel an increasing freedom to share themselves. In order to create this climate, I must demonstrate my own trust in sharing, at least some of the time, out of my own concerns. If I want the group to share in a personal way, I need to come to them on a personal level.

The focus is on the present rather than on the past, on feeling rather than on idea, on observing rather than on analyzing, on sharing rather than on solving. If someone

[4] See Robert C. Leslie, "Helping the Theological Student Dare to Be Himself," in Hans Hofmann, ed., *The Ministry and Mental Health* (New York: Association Press, 1960) , pp. 127-41.

brings up a problem he is struggling with, my task as leader is not to try to solve it, or even to understand its origin, but simply to acknowledge it, encourage full expression of it, and relate it to observed patterns of behavior. It is my responsibility to provide support when support is needed, to pursue a tentative expression of feeling until the real emotion is revealed, to protect a member when he feels under attack. It is my task, too, to challenge the group and its members toward growth, to point out learning as it is experienced, to relate incidents as experienced to the study of the Christian faith.

Student Reactions

The validity of this kind of learning experience is testified to by three students. The first is Mona, a woman working on a graduate degree in the biblical field.

Everything about my experience in this group has said to me: "This is good; this is what you need; you have discovered that life, after all, can be something for which to be grateful." Other courses in my seminary career have been interesting, even exciting, but none have given me new life or a sense of myself as a person with integrity. This would not be surprising if I had spent the last three years in a secular school, but because I have been in a seminary where I have been studying nothing but Christianity itself, I am sufficiently impressed to wonder why. Why has *this* class reached me in a way that my others

143

have not? Why have I responded to *this* class in a way that I have not responded to others?

This articulate woman attempts an answer to her own question; but before dealing with her answer, let me cite two male students who share feelings similar to hers. The first is Nick:

The primary thing which I gained from this experience was for the first time feeling important to a group, not merely because I had certain skills and talents, but because I was me, an individual who was valued for that reason alone. This was a feeling that gave me a profound sense of how the early church must have grown, how the gospel must have first been communicated, and how it can be communicated again. In many ways this was the most intensive exposure to creative *agape* love that I have ever had.

The second male student, Arch, elaborates in some detail on his perception of theological dimensions in the group experience:

We are reminded that a therapeutic group can, like the church, be a redemptive, caring, and healing community. It is a place where those who know the brokenness of illness or anxiety, of separation or hopelessness, may experience the healing powers of a loving communion of persons who reach out to embrace them. . . . Our group has become for each of us one of those mysterious

144

channels of the grace of life, and we can only feel grateful to be recipients of that grace. Yet we are called to be not only recipients, but also instruments. As we go out to other groups, as members or leaders, our call is to be effective instruments of that healing grace.

Experiencing Theology

These three students are not exceptional. They are, to be sure, better able to articulate their reactions than many, but the thrust of their testimony is shared rather generally. All three of these students were participants in classes in interpersonal relationships, classes in which a therapeutic, i.e. a growth-producing, atmosphere is encouraged within a framework of Christian commitment. Such small group experience meets several of the suggestions listed above as made by students. But even more important, this kind of group activity can become a means for experiencing theology, for living out, rather than just hearing about, theological concepts. Through students' actual participation in real life relationships within the group, theological issues are clarified as they are struggled with. Pam, in a letter reflecting on such a group experience, wrote: "I think the group was certainly representative of living theology." She elaborates her thought in these words:

One of your students wrote in a letter which you later quoted in an article that the group "got those things out of the way which keep us from loving each other." Basic theology: reconciliation. We learned to love each crooked

145

group member with our crooked hearts; theologically we were forgiven and accepted sinners. We learned to pick up our lives and kiss them [referring to Arthur Miller, *After the Fall*] instead of fleeing and hiding from ourselves (and naturally from others). I could go on elaborating, but I'm sure it's clear. Learning to love, to take responsibility, to trust life: gut-level theology.

I would like to illustrate how this "gut-level theology" finds expression in small groups by dealing with two theological concepts: grace and crucifixion. I do not mean to imply that the small group experience exhausts the meaning of these concepts, but I am suggesting that in the small group these concepts can be experienced with startling relevance.

Grace

The kind of acceptance which is typical of the small, sharing group is closely related to the theological idea of grace. Mona, whom I have quoted before, is quite explicit about this aspect of group life. She writes:

Now the goal of the group, within the class as I have perceived it, has been the enrichment of the life of each member as an individual. The method of the group has been to accept each member as he is.

There is probably no doctrine of the Christian faith harder to believe than the idea that a person is acceptable not because of the things that he does but because of the real

146

person that he is. In order to be acceptable, we have the common tendency to withhold anything of the self that is not pleasant and desirable and attractive. But the small group provides opportunity, within the supportive trust that gradually builds up, to risk sharing even the dark aspects of one's life. Pam tells of her experience of sharing and of the acceptance which she received:

> With a high degree of nonverbal support from Karl, Will, and Paul, I committed myself to the group the fourth week by relating to the group the destructive relationships I had experienced with my family. I was shaken and defensive after the group and tagged along with Karl and Arch to avoid being alone. The following day Dr. Leslie picked this up, and I was able to finish working it out. Dr. Leslie's hug at the end of the session conveyed a tremendously warm acceptance of me, and Karl succeeded in conveying a sense of support that has made me feel very close to him ever since.

The point is that in the small group many members feel an acceptance in a way they have never experienced before, and the acceptance is not only of the nice parts of their lives but of their whole beings. There has never been a time in which the need for people to be in touch with their whole selves was greater than today! The electronic revolution has transformed our concepts of time and space. Even the remote corners of the earth are readily accessible through the air waves immediately and by plane in a matter of hours. As George Leonard puts it in his book *Education and Ecstasy:*

"A world in which everyone will be in touch needs people in touch with themselves." [5] Mona notes how the small group opened the doorway to deeper personal integration for herself, an integration essential for the automated world that Marshall McLuhan writes about. I am repeating her statement about acceptance and then continuing:

> The method of the group has been to accept each member as he is, and to open the floor to honest communication. What this has meant to many in the group has been the blazing of a trail for the expression of emotion. Having been reared by mid-twentieth-century middle-class parents, we have been taught to relate to others with a minimum of emotion. We have been taught that we should ignore and mistrust our feelings because they are less valid than our thoughts. This approach has split our very beings into components of mind, emotion, and body; and we have learned to live with this split. Becoming aware of ourselves as whole beings whose mind, emotion, and body are thoroughly interrelated and equally valuable has been a significant accomplishment for many in the group; and it is a crucially important accomplishment for living in the automated world that McLuhan foretells.

When contact with the feeling level has been established, and hence a deeper sense of personal integration has been achieved, the group provides opportunity for expressing newly discovered feelings. Don writes of his experience as follows:

[5] (New York: Delacorte Press, 1968), p. 127.

I began to feel an acceptance from the group. Once feeling this acceptance, I felt freer to express myself. A loving climate was encouraged not only verbally but through physical expression. Pam has told the group again and again how much it meant for her to be hugged by Bob [the leader]. This involved some risk on his part, I am sure, but it helped others of us talk about expressing and accepting affection as well as feeling more free to express ourselves in this way.

A good deal of interest in any small, sharing group held under church auspices tends to center around hostile feelings. As has already been indicated, hostility has been frowned on in the Christian culture. The result is that when hostile feelings are encouraged, they sometimes come out with unexpected force, often with earthy Anglo-Saxon language. Don notes how his group handled their hostility:

We learned that we could express our feelings openly, even feelings of hostility. On the day Bob was late to class, Will suggested that the last chair be removed from the room so Bob would come in and find that he had no chair. This may well have been all in fun, but the point is that Bob showed us that we can be free enough to even invite hostile feelings. Later in the session Bob asked if Will might not have suggested hiding the chair because he had hostile feelings toward the leader. The issue was brought out into the open where it could be dealt with creatively. I don't think that our group ever enjoyed hostility. We learned, however, not to be afraid of it.

An excerpt from the tape recording of this group session demonstrates how the issue was brought out into the open. In the process of dealing with hostile feelings, the strategic importance of a relationship with the leader is made clear. Pam is responding to Leslie (the leader) :

Pam: I'd like to ask a question about a transaction that went between you and Will about hostility and devilment.

Leslie: Yeah, I think it's appropriate. There's some unfinished business there. (*Laughter when two start to talk at once.*)

Pam: Devilment like the chair . . . and Dr. Leslie said: "Isn't that hospitality?" then, well, never finished it.

Leslie: (*role-playing Will, in a loud tone of voice.*) "I'm going to show that guy. When he comes into the room there's not going to be any place for him to sit and he's going to be real embarrassed and real upset. I'll fix him, I will, I will." (*Some quiet laughter.*) Devilry?

Nick: I felt it some.

Someone: I didn't feel it that way.

Leslie: How did you feel it, Will? Go ahead and exaggerate it as much as I did.

Will: I just never thought of it. (*Laughter.*) It makes me wonder how much of the fun I have in life is hostility. It's a sort of a habit. You mean, I do it because I'm hostile? Are these hidden feelings that are coming out this way?

Leslie: Well, let's make use of the group. What about the response? This was Will's suggestion, apparently, that—ah—there be no chair for Leslie when he comes in. How did it impress you?

Don: I didn't . . . I thought for one thing . . . I think I thought of you more as a member of the group, giving too much prominence by making such a big thing of it.

Leslie: You mean it wasn't important one way or another.

Don: Yeah . . . I . . . I thought you were playing a game with us, and—ah—I don't want to get off the subject here too much, but you say you're not playing games, and this relaxes me more. I don't mind playing games, I think, but I just don't like to be outsmarted. (*Laughter.*) Sometimes I think you do play games.

Leslie: Some explanation is needed there. We'll come back to that.

Don: OK. That's OK. That's unfinished business. Anyway, that's how I reacted, I think, to that. "Don't make a big deal about it, Arch, go ahead, and don't worry about where he's going to sit." But you, Dr. Leslie, are pretty important to me, I think.

(Will talks about his experiences with hostility, then Pam comes in.)

Pam: I really do think it's hostility, I was really stopped by what you said, 'cause I was going right along with you, Will, thinking it was just fun. It really stopped me.

Leslie: Yes, I think it's hostile because I don't know what the message is.

Will: It's hostile to you.

Leslie: It's hostile when I don't know what the message is. Then we explore it and discover that the message is just fun—but at the moment, when I come in the room and there's no chair, I don't know what this means. And if I don't know what it means, then it makes me anxious. And if I'm made anxious, it has been a hostile approach to the situation. But we worked it out. We talked about it. We looked at it. We came back to it and sort of walked around it and I discover that you think of it as sheer fun. I'm also pointing out that—ah—maybe what is sheer fun to you gets interpreted different ways by others.

Pam: Yeah, I took the ball away from you, too, Arch. What were you going to say about moving the chairs out into the hall?

Arch: No, I was sort of . . . I think I was—ah— I thought that Dr. Leslie's interpretation was right. Each of us saw this in a different way. And I know that my suggestion that we—ah

—that we move all the chairs out into the hall . . . it was a ridiculous suggestion. (*Laughter.*) On the other hand . . . on the other hand, I'm sure that a part of this was my apprehension about where you were, and why hadn't you come, and . . .

Leslie: "I'll fix him."

Will: He'll have to sit in the hall. (*Laughter.*) Well, how much of joking and fun is always a product of this thing?

Leslie: Well, it's ambiguous, you see. It's not a clear message. That's what we've been talking about all morning.

The importance of this excerpt is not just that negative feelings could be explored, but that the person with negative feelings was still accepted in spite of his feelings. *All* of him was accepted. The group had become, as Arch wrote, "one of those mysterious channels of the grace of life."

Grace, i.e. unearned love, as a concept is virtually impossible to understand except as it has been experienced. When a person has felt accepted even when his behavior did not warrant it, he has begun to sense what God's acceptance is like. The sharing group provides a natural medium for being a vehicle of acceptance which approximates grace.

Crucifixion

In a similar way the small interacting group can help its members to understand crucifixion on an experiential level. When people speak of participation in a sensitivity group as a "religious experience," they are really referring to a feeling of rebirth, to a dying to old self and an affirming of new relationships. Reuel Howe reminds us of how lovers would like to avoid the pain of adjusting to each other, but as he says, "The full meaning of their love cannot become available to them except as they pass through the challenges and crises of their relationship and die to themselves for the sake of the other." [6]

For all too many Christians, crucifixion is only an event in history that climaxed the ministry of Jesus of Nazareth. But if crucifixion is to have meaning to man today, it needs to be seen not only as a historic event but also as a continuing experience. Crucifixion means that the forces working in life for good are being struck down constantly by the powers of evil, as experienced by Jesus. Crucifixion involves the recognition of hostility as a regular part of life which needs to be faced and dealt with and worked through. Reuel Howe points to the commonness in everyday life of crucifixion:

The Christian fellowship, therefore, is the fellowship of men and women who accept dying as a part of living, and who are not surprised by the presence in human relations of selfishness, betrayals, misrepresentations, hostility and all other violations of the ideal. When we meet these things, we should not run away, or pretend that such

[6] Howe, *Herein Is Love* (Valley Forge, Pa.: Judson Press, 1961), p. 38.

conditions do not exist. Instead, we should face these hostile and negative human responses with courage.[7]

The small, sharing group is one of the few places where the hurt of life can really be examined. In a group which I recently led, one of the members became quite angry with me when I would not fight with him. Goaded by his persistent attack, I finally responded angrily and clobbered him into submission. It was only after he had withdrawn that I sensed what I had done. His overtures which I had interpreted as attack were only his clumsy efforts at establishing a closer relationship. Reaching out toward the leader, in what he interpreted as a positive gesture, had met with almost total rejection. Here he experienced a kind of crucifixion. It now became my task, and the group's task, to demonstrate to him that we could grow together through the pain of this experience. Throughout the remainder of the group sessions his relationship with me and with the group was a focal point. We had participated together in a crucifixion-like experience, and we were all caught up in its pain. But the very effort at talking about it, at re-examining it, at working on overtures to heal the hurt, spoke of crucifixion as a common experience in life.

There is no better place than in the small, sharing group for learning that growth comes through facing pain. Arch writes of the parellel between the sharing group (with therapeutic overtones) and the church:

We seldom realize that a therapeutic group is . . . like

[7] *Ibid.,* p. 39.

the church, a confessional community. Its members come laden with their own guilt, their own sense of inadequacy, their own feeling of estrangement from others, and their own need to reveal themselves and feel acceptance.

It is the guilts, the inadequacies, and the estrangements that create the interpersonal problems, that lead constantly to crucifixion. It is one of the privileges of the small group to demonstrate that hurts can be tolerated, that growth comes through pain, that crucifixion is followed by resurrection. Experience on the man-to-man level adds new insight into the man-to-God relationship.

Learning Through Personal Involvement

The theological concepts that can be understood through experience in the small group might be extended almost indefinitely. The point is that learning takes place best, in theological concepts as well as in every other area, when the learner is personally involved. And personal involvement calls for attention to what is happening in the current life of the learner. Just as this involvement is possible in the teaching-learning process described in this book, so it is possible in the small, sharing group. It is to be noted, however, that involvement is essential not only for the group member but for the leader as well. Just as this book has constantly stressed the use that the counselor makes of himself, so the group leader has as his chief tool his own use of himself.

I have pointed out the positive impact of my hug in

demonstrating to Pam that I did indeed accept her. I have noted, too, how my clumsy handling of a needy student, who sought a relationship with me in a forthright and aggressive manner, led to a feeling of rejection so severe that it seemed like crucifixion to him. And I have hinted at how painful the process of attempting reconciliation was, and how much energy I needed to expend in trying to undo the harm done. The pain of growth, referred to in earlier chapters of this volume, was very real here. But the joy of reconciliation was there, too—the sense of a new relationship, the confidence that good could emerge out of the bad. While we did not deliberately set out to accomplish therapy, healing did take place. Without the use of a single theological term, the deepest kind of theology was experienced.

One student writing appreciatively of the psychological-theological growth which she had experienced in the interpersonal relationship class declared: "I believe that my group therapy class was my most successful class because it is education that is right for right now."

This student underscored the factor that made the group valuable. The experience was *right for right now*. It had an immediate relevance because it was so close to where the student was living. And when the immediate relevance is related to the larger dimensions of faith, it is a combination hard to beat. In such a setting the legitimate needs of the new type of theological student can be met.

9

Reality Practice in a Pastoral Counseling Course with Student Supervision

Robert A. Nykamp

Professor Nykamp describes his attempts in a seminary setting to create a classroom situation which has some of the features of a clinical experience. His example of "reality practice" demonstrates how theological students can learn about themselves and about counseling skills through a modified role-playing approach.

Robert A. Nykamp is Director of Counseling and Assistant Professor of Christian Ministry at Western Theological Seminary (Reformed), Holland, Michigan. He served as chairman of the committee of NIMH Fellows which developed this book.

When faced with the task of teaching a classroom course in pastoral counseling, you ask yourself how these men may have a taste of the kind of teaching-learning experience they would gain from a training program under supervision, such as has been described in the early chapters of this book. The problem is heightened by such factors as (a) an instructor-student ratio of 1 to 30 rather than 1 to 15; (b) scheduled meetings with the students three hours weekly for three months rather than eight hours weekly for nine months; (c) a lack of ready clients in a supervised clinical setting; (d) students with a variety of backgrounds, a diversity of abilities and experiences, and a great many fears about becoming involved in ministry.

This chapter describes an attempt to transfer the supervised teaching-learning experience into the seminary classroom through the use of a method sometimes called "reality practice," to which I was introduced by Howard Clinebell.[1]

Pattern for Reality Practice

In this instance, the entire class of thirty students was divided into ten groups with three students in each. The students established their own groups, thereby having an opportunity to choose the persons with whom they felt most comfortable. One hour each week was spent in the reality practice session, with all ten groups meeting in small circles in the same room. The groups usually remained constant for the entire eleven-week quarter unless students desired to make a change. The type of role presented in each group was often related to specific content and counseling methods studied during the week.

Many students need assistance in the first experiences in reality practice, both with the role playing and the counseling. The instructor can give assistance as he moves from one group to the other and can help the groups share with the entire class problems encountered, responses and methods found helpful, and difficulties uncovered which prevented the development of helpful relationships.

One student begins by taking the role of an individual

[1] Howard J. Clinebell, Jr., *Basic Types of Pastoral Counseling* (Nashville: Abingdon Press, 1966), pp. 25-26.

with whom he has counseled or whose "life world" he knows rather well. It is important that the student think very specifically about this person and identify as fully as possible with the person's style of life, attitudes, beliefs, assumptions, expectations, and feelings. This gives the seminarian who takes the role (R) an opportunity to sit where the other sits, and it helps him develop an empathic understanding of the situation of the hypothetical client.

Another student is to relate to this person as a pastoral counselor (PC). He is to be himself in the role of the counselor, as natural and real as possible. This is a difficult task, and I find many students unable to achieve this role until they have had a number of experiences in reality practice. The third student is an observer-evaluator (OE). He is responsible for recording key exchanges in the conversation, evaluating responses of the pastor, and keeping account of time.

I have found it is best for students to participate in a reality practice dialogue for about ten minutes and then to discuss what took place. The three participants can discuss the feelings each had, the responses which they felt were helpful in the counseling process, the attitudes or approaches which hindered, and the interpersonal dynamics. Appropriate goals in counseling can be established and the reality practice dialogue can then be continued for another ten to fifteen minutes, followed again by evaluative discussion.

Ideally at this time the pastoral counselor (PC) or observer-evaluator (OE) should know the life world of the person being counseled well enough to take the role (R) and let the first student do the counseling. In this switching of roles, the student can also have practice in counseling the person seeking help as well as putting himself into the life world of another person.

Reality Practice Dialogue 1

This process can best be illustrated with excerpts from a taped reality practice experience of three seminary students, one of whom is working for his Th.M. degree and two of whom have had experiences in clinical pastoral education and are involved in a graduate theological degree program. After the students have moved beyond this basic course, they often meet for their own practice sessions and consult me later.

The following is from a warm-up dialogue. One student begins:

I'll play the role of a girl, Mary, whom I have been trying to help for about one and one-half years. Mary grew up in a sheltered home environment and is twenty-one years old. About two years ago Mary became involved with a young black, Ben. They spent a great deal of time together and Mary eventually became pregnant.

Mary went to live with Ben, which caused a break between her and her family. Her parents did not and still do not want to see her. She is not married and never has been. Now she is living with Ben in a common-law marriage and she is pregnant.

Mary is an immigrant to this country and was brought

161

up in a very conservative, traditional church. I, as Mary, will come to you, Pastor.

After this warm-up the reality practice dialogue begins:

Mary 1:   Hi, Pastor. I called you a little earlier because I really want to see you. I'm kind of in trouble.

Pastor 1:   Be seated, Mary. What's the problem? (*Harsh.*)

Mary 2:   You see, Pastor, I'm pregnant and I'm not married. And my folks are pretty upset. And that wouldn't even be so bad, but the guy by whom I'm pregnant is black. (*Pause.*) We've known each other for about four or five months. He was living with some college students, and a couple of my girl friends and I used to go over there, you know, just to visit the guys. But this guy's wife and his kids ran out on him and he was really lonely and I wanted to do something for him. I wanted to help him out. But I guess we got too close.

Pastor 2:   You were lonely, too, huh?

Mary 3:   Yeah. (*Silence.*)

Pastor 3:   Tell me, Mary. What is your relationship with your parents at this time? What I'm trying to ask you is—well, let's go back. Are you living with this man still?

Mary 4:   Yeah, I am. My parents don't want me in the house anymore.

Pastor 4:   That is what I was . . .

Mary 5:   (*Interrupts.*) You see, sir, for a while there —at first I used to visit him all the time. Then one of the youth ministers of our church talked to Ben and Ben spilled the whole story to him, and I had to tell my parents something about it. After that they were really upset and they told my brothers and sisters. My brother came up from Indiana and got me out of that house where Ben was living and with two of my sisters took me down to Florida. My brother thought it would be good if I got out of this situation to think it over. But when we were there, he really got rough with me and a couple of times he physically attacked me. So when we came back up here, I just decided that I was going to move out of the house to live with Ben. I don't want to have anything to do with my brother anymore. He and I are through. I don't want to see him again. I'm dead scared of him. And my folks take his side. No, I just can't live at home anymore. I (*sigh*) . . . I just don't care to live at home anymore because if he shows up there, he might just kill me.

Pastor 5:   What I hear you saying, Mary, is you don't want anything to do with your folks, you

163

are living with Ben. But I feel you're saying, "I want Ben and my parents too."

Mary 6: Yeah, because I love my parents too. I don't want to hurt them.

Pastor 6: This is a real dilemma, huh? The old pressure from both sides. How do you feel about being pregnant with Ben?

Mary 7: I feel pretty happy about that. The part of the thing that complicates it is that he's still legally married to his wife. He's not divorced. His wife lives in Texas and she's supposed to start divorce proceedings. I don't think she has, yet. Ben isn't doing anything about it.

Pastor 7: Um-hum.

Mary 8: So, I don't know what is going to happen, but Ben wants to get divorced from his wife and I think after that we can get married. But my parents are really upset about the fact that I've been living with a married man, that I'm pregnant by a married man. But I think it will really help Ben and me to get along together. It will tie us closer together.

Recognition of Difficulties

The conversation continues with the pastor being inappropriately confronting and interpreting.

He tells Mary he believes her parents have a right to be angry, that she is not having any guilt, that the difficulty is really between her and her parents, and that she is trying to exert her independence through her behavior.

Mary continues to plead with the pastor for help, asking for understanding and assistance in reaching her parents. She reveals that she is the youngest of the family and that she had a serious leg infection which continued for almost a year. At this time she felt her parents really cared for her.

In the classroom use of reality practice the instructor needs to help the students stop after brief intervals to talk about what has taken place in the interview. There is a tendency on the part of students working alone to avoid evaluative discussion. They seem to operate out of the feeling that it is rather painful to discuss what they have done, and that if only they work with the situation a little longer, they can solve it. It can be the observer-evaluator's task to call time and to invite discussion.

In this instance, R and OE could have told PC he was not very understanding with his second response (P-2). For example, he could have been more helpful in building a relationship if he had said instead, "You wanted to help Ben in his loneliness, and this resulted in your becoming pregnant and then later a break with your parents." Mary could then, hopefully, have been able to share more of her feelings instead of blocking with a "Yeah" and silence. This I shared with one of the students when I discussed the tape with him.

The reality practice dialogue continues:

Mary 22:   I don't really want to get at my parents. I
             don't want to use Ben for that. I don't *really*

	want to use Ben for that. I don't *really* use Ben for that.
Pastor 22:	You want to prove that you can make it on your own. Prove that you're independent. Prove that you're an adult.
Mary 23:	That's part of it.
Pastor 23:	Show your parents that they're wrong and that you're not a child.
Mary 24:	Then they should be able to accept me as I am, what I'm doing. I know, the way things have turned out, it isn't good.
Pastor 24:	Do you expect your parents to accept you right now? You're having trouble accepting yourself.
Mary 25:	I don't understand that. I don't know what you mean by that.
Pastor 25:	Why did you come here? Are you ready just to accept the situation? You know, what you're saying is, "Okay, if my parents can't accept Ben, that's the way it is, but I'm not going to let them stand in my way, so no problem." You know? Live with Ben until he gets his divorce and then marry him. But that's not true; there is a problem. The problem is inside of you.
Mary 26:	Well, I want to be able to go home. I want to be able to talk to my dad and mom. I need help right now.
Pastor 26:	What do you need help for, Mary?
Mary 27:	I want to be able to keep that baby. I want

to be able to bring it up myself. Because I feel I can do it. I want to do it. Because that baby's going to be mine. People are looking at me and they're saying, "You know, there goes that girl." I'm not going to be able to continue working too much longer because it's beginning to show and people know that I'm single. It's not good for a single girl to run around pregnant.

Pastor 27:   Mary, is that what you think of yourself, too? There goes *that* girl?

Mary 28:   No, that's me. It's too bad. That's tough. That's me. This is the situation I'm in. I don't know how I'm going to get through it. I don't know how I'm going to be able to face everybody, but that's me.

Pastor 28:   What do you mean, that's me?

Mary 29:   That's the situation that I'm in right now. There's no way out. I'm scared because I don't know if I'll be able to have the baby with my bad leg and all that. I don't know how it's going to turn out, but this is what I want now. Since I'm in this situation now I want to be able to go through with it. I'm going to!

Pastor 29:   You're not very convincing.

Mary 30:   That's tough!

Pastor 30:   I hear a girl saying, "I want my mother to put her arms around me. I'm scared. I want

167

my father to show that he loves me. I need
him."

Mary 31: Go on. Okay. I am scared. I really am afraid.
And I want my mother to be able to say that
to me.

Observer 1: Let's cut and discuss the situation.

First Discussion by Students

In the first round of discussion, the observer commented
that he feels the pastor and Mary are not always dealing in
the primary relationships. He was rather critical of the pastor
saying that he has not explored at all how Mary feels about
Ben and how Ben feels about her; he believes that she
probably feels threatened in her relationship with Ben, and
he noticed she qualifies every statement about Ben. However, the PC was not able to accept the observation of the
OE, and he insisted that he feels the main difficulty is in
the conflict between Mary and her parents. He argued that
it is necessary to explore this conflict before they can talk
at all about the relationship with Ben. R agreed with the PC,
and the PC went on to say he felt it necessary to make
R become defensive and angry before he could really identify
with Mary's feelings. R was so much in the role that prac-
tically all the discussion is with the PC while still in the
role; R continued to speak in the first person and to share
a cry for help and a plea for understanding. In the first
discussion session the OE was not given an opportunity
to make any more observations, and the PC and R continued to talk with each other and finally decided to con-

tinue with a second session of reality practice dialogue.

The PC stated that at one or two spots in the dialogue he didn't know who he was, and that the sequence of events in Mary's life was often confusing to him. The discussion of the dialogue helped him to move more clearly into his role.

In talking with the student R about this discussion period from the tape, I tried to help him look at the interaction in the small group. R recognized he had identified with Mary so fully he could not separate himself from her. He also could not confront the student who was the PC with his feelings of being inferior to him.

The second session of reality practice began with a different approach, and the pastor seemed to feel more comfortable and more understanding. This new attitude apparently developed in the student discussion period.

Reality Practice Dialogue 2

Pastor 1: Mary, I get the feeling you sense the pressure of wanting your parents to love you and yet feel their rejection. I feel a whole lot of ambivalence. Do you know what that term means?

Mary 1: Yeah! You feel two ways about it.

Pastor 2: Two equal and opposite feelings, of wanting so badly to accept yourself. "This is the way I am; I'm going to be an adult in this situation. I'm going to handle it." On the other side of the coin you say, "I want my mother and father to care for me and take care of me and love me." Pretty lonely gal, aren't you?

Mary 2: I feel lonely right now. Very much so. I go grabbing around for help and it just doesn't come anywhere. And the help I'm looking for is for somebody to say, "Okay, okay, you're in a tough situation, but I'll stick with you, I'll stick with you." Right now, Ben's out of work. He sits alone in the house.

Pastor 3: That's no good.

Mary 3: You know, he gets all upset about the fact that he isn't bringing home any money. Well, after a while we probably won't know where the next meal is coming from. And then he's worried about the fact that he's not taking care of me and I don't get the proper food, and that doesn't help me any either.

Pastor 4: Nobody is meeting your needs, are they?

Mary 4: Not right now. But it helps a little bit to sit here and talk about it, but I still have to go through the whole thing myself.

Pastor 5: That's right. And I get the feeling you'd like me to say, "Okay, I'll go convince your folks it's all right," and I can't do that.

Mary 5: No, I don't suppose. Because they went to their minister. You know, they went to church, and I guess he's on their side.

Pastor 6: Is that the way it is, sides? In this corner we have Mary, in that corner we have the rest of the world.

Mary 6:   I don't know about the rest of the world. The rest of *my* world.

Pastor 7:   Yeah! Wow! That's pretty lonely.

Mary 7:   What can we do about it?

Pastor 8:   Let's look at some very real things. You need your parents.

Mary 8:   Yeah!

Pastor 9:   Right! You want them.

Mary 9:   Right!

Pastor 10: And yet, right now neither one of them is meeting your need.

Mary 10:   Right!

Opportunity for Self-Awareness

I had previously worked with R on verbatims he had written of two counseling sessions with Mary. At that time R found it difficult to focus on Mary's feelings about herself, about her parents, and about her situation. but in playing the role of Mary, R had experienced some of Mary's feelings, and was helped in the student discussion that took place to identify the importance of the pastor's focus on client feelings. He could now go back to his counseling with Mary with some new awareness and goals. Even though a skilled supervisor could find many more areas to improve in both the counseling process and the student discussion, a student was able to teach another student a very crucial lesson in counseling—to *listen for* and *respond to* the client's feelings.

At this time the students were not able to specify goals

or decide exactly how the counselor should proceed. However, it can be seen that in this experience there was a sharing of insight and feelings and that each person was able to make some discoveries about himself and about the counseling process.

Thus, even in such limited training settings as reality practice in a classroom, students learn from each other and may help each other develop greater awareness of the way they use themselves in counseling situations.

Objectives and Use of Evaluation

This brief illustration points to a way of incorporating some of the teaching-learning process experienced in supervised training into a seminary course, at least in an introductory way. Through the dramatization of situations which actually arise in the student's field education experience, and through evaluative reflection upon those situations, the developing minister may be assisted in becoming more effective in his helping relationships. Under guidance from the instructor, who meets with each reality practice group in rotation, the students provide each other with a degree of supervision, thus assisting each other in developing skill in their counseling relationships. The use of tape recording and careful review of each session are added resources in their learning.

To clarify for students the goals of this experience, and to assist both students and myself as we collaborate in the evaluation process, I have prepared the following educational objectives for the course:

to experience as well as describe the process
of pastoral counseling;
to explore the relationship between pastoral
counseling and other aspects of ministry;
to introduce students to some of the basic
types of pastoral counseling;
to develop an increasing awareness of the
student's attitudes toward persons, including himself;
to help the student analyze this ability to
establish meaningful relationships;
to identify and illustrate different ways to
respond to a person's verbal communication;
to introduce the student to a working understanding of personality classifications;
to help the student grow in skill in using himself in a helping relationship;
to help the student to integrate his theological
stance within his helping relationships;
to suggest ways to assist individuals in the Christian
community to experience movement toward wholeness.

Each student is expected to write a brief self-evaluation using the course objectives as a base. The following three quotations from student evaluation papers share some of their thoughts about the reality practice method:

We had not been doing reality practice very long when my counselee made an important observation to me. He said I was tense in the counselor role. I appeared to be trying to do something for him, rather than listening to him. I thought about that for a while and discovered I was so engrossed in counseling techniques that I was not showing empathy and understanding to the counselee. I find I am usually relaxed when I talk to people, no matter how formal the occasion, but as a counselor I often fall into the trap of becoming too technique conscious. I am now trying to give more of myself in every response. I believe I am discovering myself as a person-counselor rather than as a technique-counselor.

I was able in reality practice to demonstrate some skill in using myself in a helping relationship. Frankly, I surprised myself most of all in this area of the course. I believe I have the potential to become a good counselor, and I intend to do my best to develop fully this talent. At certain times during reality practice I also became aware of my increased ability to recognize my own limitations in helping relationships and to make proper referrals. I could permit another student to counsel with "my" parishioner when I recognized he could do a better job.

I believe certain areas of the course might have been discussed more in class rather than spending about one third of the time in reality practice. Yet, if more data had been related, I would not have been able to learn all I did about myself. Counseling is the skill of relating to others, not a systematic computerization of a man to recite data and method. I believe I might have learned more *about* counseling if the course had been conducted in a different way, but I would not have learned anything about *being* a counselor. This is what I learned.

10

Practical Examples of Continuing Education

Howard J. Clinebell, Jr.

Stressing the strategic importance of the case-study approach, and noting the crucial significance of direct one-to-one supervision, Dr. Clinebell describes many new patterns of continuing education in pastoral counseling. In his position as Professor of Pastoral Counseling at the School of Theology at Claremont (Methodist), Claremont, California, Dr. Clinebell has been particularly concerned about meeting the needs of parish ministers. Programs referred to in this chapter are all ones in which he has participated at Claremont, unless otherwise indicated.

Howard J. Clinebell, Jr. was one of the guiding spirits behind the founding of the American Association of Pastoral Counselors and was its first president. He is the author of several books: Basic Types of Pastoral Counseling *(Abingdon Press, 1966)*, Mental Health Through Christian Community *(Abingdon Press, 1965)*, Understanding and Counseling the Alcoholic *(Abingdon Press, 1968)*, *with Harvey Seifert*, Personal Growth and Social Change *(Westminster Press, 1969)*, *and, with Charlotte H. Clinebell*, The Intimate Marriage *(Harper & Row, 1970)*.

"Nowadays it is so hard to stay ahead of reality. Let us assume the future will surprise us." [1]

Effective clergymen today must continue to grow in their

---

[1] George B. Leonard, *Education and Ecstasy*, p. 16.

professional skills. Only thus can they stay ahead of the changing realities of family life in the surprising world which is continually emerging. Innovative styles of continuing education are crucially needed to facilitate lifelong learning. The variety of such programs which have already been developed in pastoral counseling is exciting and hopeful. This chapter describes a few of these. The purpose is to stimulate the creativity of persons designing continuing education programs. The needs and interests of clergymen vary tremendously; therefore, a network of programs in many different settings, modeled on a variety of patterns, is needed.

Primary responsibility for continuing clergy education rests with those institutions which exist to train ministers—the theological schools. These graduate professional schools are both the basic training centers and the "think tanks" of the churches. If continuing pastoral education is to stay connected with the mainstream of creative theological developments and relevant to the life of the churches, seminaries must take increased initiative in this field. But continuing education involving supervised training must also be available in an increasing number of nonseminary settings—pastoral counseling centers, mental health services, local churches, clinical pastoral training centers, denominational and ecumenical settings, marriage counseling centers, etc. In this way training can become available on a broad enough basis geographically to release the tremendous counseling potential of our country's 364,000 priests, rabbis, and pastors. The examples which follow illustrate several patterns of sponsorship, setting, and design.

Seminary Courses

Most theological schools offer several courses in pastoral counseling. Since approximately 60 percent of all counseling by pastors deals with family problems, this is a prominent emphasis in such courses. Collectively these courses represent a major resource for continuing clergy education. Their usefulness in this regard can be enhanced if these guidelines are followed by seminaries:

The availability of the courses should be systematically publicized in ministerial circles.

Parish clergymen should be encouraged to enroll by scheduling the courses on a one-day-per-week basis.

The maximum use should be made of the more dynamic teaching methods such as the analysis of verbatims and tapes of counseling sessions (preferably by the class members), skill practice sessions (role-playing of new counseling approaches),[2] plunge experiences (supervised intensive exposure to persons in crisis in institutions), and professional growth groups.

Practicing clergymen are even more resistant than theological students to less dynamic teaching methods, particularly to the older didactic lecture approach.

Enrollment of ministers in seminary courses on a "refresher" basis is encouraged by the Southern California–Arizona Conference of The United Methodist Church, which asks its churches to give their pastors one day a week for

[2] See chap. IX on "reality practice."

177

continuing education courses. (This day is in addition to the ministers' day off each week for recreational and family activities.) Several seminaries have helped to establish professional associations to stimulate motivation in continuing education among parish ministers.[8]

A course at a California seminary entitled "Major Counseling Opportunities of the Minister" illustrates this type of opportunity. Beginning with the pastoral care and counseling opportunities with expectant parents and parents of infants, this course focuses successively on each of Erikson's eight developmental stages. It emphasizes both family life education and counseling. Following this, it surveys the counseling opportunities related to the major crises which hit families—sickness, bereavement, mental illness, alcoholism. Approximately one third of the course (which totals four hours a week for sixteen weeks) is used in lab sessions employing case material, tapes of pastoral counseling interviews, and role-playing. All students keep a "log" for recording insights and growth experiences from their skill practice sessions. These are weekly meetings in terms of three students, outside of class. The instructor rotates among these practice sessions to provide supervision.

How desirable is it to mix theological students and parish clergymen? The professional generation gap poses problems, but it has also proved to be a stimulus to learning. The ministers have had counseling experiences which enrich

[8] Several seminaries in Ohio have cooperated in establishing an Academy of the Parish Ministry; the School of Theology at Claremont has worked with a group of ministers in setting up an Academy for Continuing Theological Studies.

class interaction. Furthermore, they take the course because of a sense of need. They are highly motivated by knowing firsthand the perils and frustrations of lack of training in counseling. With some theologs, their enthusiasm is contagious.

Seminary-Staffed Extension Courses

Courses taught on seminary campuses are available only to ministers within commuting distance and those who have a study sabbatical from their churches (a sprinkling of enlightened churches are granting such blocks of three months to a year for "retreading" experiences). To increase continuing education opportunities, several seminaries have set up off-campus courses in areas where no seminaries exist.

One seminary moved its entire summer school, including courses in pastoral care, to a city in another state.[4] This project was co-sponsored by the state leadership of the denomination with which the school is identified.

Western Theological Seminary in Holland, Michigan, combined the in-field location with the intensive institute format, sponsoring Pastoral Academic Renewal Institutes at two out-of-state centers. One of these institutes featured the combined teaching of two professors, one in church history and the other in pastoral care and counseling. The institute lasted for five days; it included a class in new approaches to pastoral counseling and an integration seminar dealing with case material brought by the ministers. Free time was

[4] Pacific School of Religion in Berkeley, California, moved its summer school to Hawaii for one summer!

available for study, recreation, relaxation, and consultation with the faculty members. Significantly, the cross-discipline teaching proved to be so valuable that the two professors are now co-teaching a course in church history and pastoral counseling in the regular curriculum of their school.

Another pattern for in-field courses calls for a seminary teacher to travel to a centrally located church six times during a sixteen-week semester for all-day classes. Distance from the school has ranged from fifty to nine hundred miles. Ministers of various denominations in an area take the initiative in requesting particular courses to meet their needs. Pastoral marriage counseling is one of the fields in which requests for courses come from ministers with considerable frequency. Courses can be audited or taken for academic credit. In several cases these extension courses have awakened a clergyman's interest in pursuing further training in counseling at the seminary or elsewhere. For example, one rabbi who took an extension course subsequently enrolled for a professional doctorate at the seminary. Upon completion of this degree, he was instrumental in establishing an interfaith pastoral counseling center in his community.

Intensive Institutes

Month-long intensive courses for Navy chaplains have been held in Philadelphia since 1965. The first course which was staffed by Marriage Council of Philadelphia had as its theme "Relationship: The Medium of Help."

Twenty-five chaplains attended. The goal was "helping the chaplain increase his skills in relationships with other Navy personnel, using himself to establish a relationship of openness, permissiveness, understanding, and acceptance with those he sees every day on-the-job and those who are troubled and come to him for help." The increase in the chaplains' counseling skills was seen as having four inseparable components:

(1) The chaplain's development of adequate knowledge of personality growth and the dynamics of human behavior, (2) the chaplain's capacity to use this knowledge in specific situations, (3) the chaplain's awareness of his own attitudes, feelings, and values as they affect the counseling relationships, and (4) the chaplain's development of a controlled use of his capacity to relate himself to the needs of the client or parishioner.

Four one-and-one-half-hour sessions per day were held five days a week. Two sessions were devoted to lectures by various resource people. One morning session was used for discussion interaction; this provided opportunity for the men to react to the guest lecturers and interact around their reading and the issues related to their role as chaplains. Daily afternoon discussion sessions were used for case analysis, role-playing, and observing live counseling interviews by members of the faculty. Strong esprit de corps developed among the chaplains as a result of their living and learning together. A study of the results of the total experience showed that the course "had been effective in profoundly influencing the professional development" of participants.[5]

On the West Coast a similar course for Navy chaplains is sponsored by a cluster of seminaries.[6] Obviously, this format could well be adapted for use with parish ministers.

A two-week intensive workshop held each summer at one seminary illustrates another pattern within this general category.

The theme of this workshop is "New Developments in Marriage and Family Counseling." The workshop meets each afternoon from 1:00 to 5:25 plus two evenings each week. Mornings are reserved for film-viewing, study, and reality practice sessions. The last evening session is a celebration. Afternoon sessions are structured to include a lecture-discussion period, a skill practice session, and a "self-other awareness" (sensitivity) group. In the latter experience the class is divided into groups of ten. One of the most productive group sessions is usually the "mini-marathon" lasting for six hours one evening. Topics considered in the course include new understandings of family interaction and conflict; communication problems in marriage; role-relationship couple counseling; conjoint family counseling; marital growth groups; retreats and marathons for couples; group methods of premarital preparation; counseling the single

[5] Herbert G. Zerof, "Relationship the Medium of Help" (Washington, D.C.: Chief of Chaplains, Bureau of Naval Personnel, October, 1968), pp. 3, 5, 20. In addition to directing this course, Dr. Zerof, a NIMH Fellow, has participated regularly in other training programs for the Navy.

[6] At the Graduate Theological Union, Berkeley, California, directed by NIMH Fellow Robert C. Leslie.

parent; counseling for remarriage; counseling ghetto families; new insights for helping the alcoholic's family; theological dimensions of marriage; and the minister's own marriage and family.

An innovative format for intensive training workshops has been developed by the Lutheran Church—Missouri Synod for use on a national scale. The demonstration pilot programs focused on both marriage counseling and education. Two four-day training sessions, approximately six to eight weeks apart, were preceded by a program of directed reading and followed by a program of ongoing guidance and evaluation. The long period between sessions was designed to enable the ministers to practice methods learned at the first session. The second session provided opportunities to discuss the results of this and to explore individual needs and problems. Each four-day session included at least ten hours of small group experience, led by a clinically trained pastor. These groups provided opportunity for practicing the art of pastoral conversation and for working through problems in relating.

Eighteen of the seminary teachers who participated in the NIMH training project at Marriage Council of Philadelphia have subsequently conducted family life conferences or career development institutes for Air Force chaplains in Europe and Asia. Emphasis on marriage counseling skills and on crisis intervention techniques proved to be especially relevant to this group of clergymen. The institutes were full time for five days. The Air Force takes continuing education for its chaplains seriously, providing one such experience per year for every chaplain.

Clinically Based Continuing Education

The advantages of clinically based programs accrue from having an opportunity to observe and/or to do marriage and family counseling under supervision. The network of some two hundred accredited clinical pastoral education centers around the country[7] provides continuing education for some clergymen, although the majority of those in CPE are theological students. Many of the more than two hundred church-related counseling centers have also developed training programs for clergymen in their areas. Because of their wide geographic distribution and their trained chaplain supervisors (supervising pastoral counselors), these two types of settings provide a major and growing resource for continuing education. The increasing number of specialists in pastoral counseling constitute a rich new source of teachers and supervisors in continuing education programs. Over four hundred clergymen have qualified for membership in AAPC.[8] Each of these persons is an active or potential teach-

[7] Accredited by the Association for Clinical Pastoral Education.

[8] The American Association of Pastoral Counselors is the accrediting agency for ministers with advanced training in pastoral counseling. Within the past decade pastoral counseling has emerged as a specialty within the ministry. (It continues to be an important function of the general parish minister, of course.) Specialists engage in full-time ministries of teaching and practicing counseling in a variety of settings. Some are ministers of pastoral care in large churches with multiple staffs. Others are employed in directing or staffing the growing number of church-related counseling programs. Some function in community mental health centers as clergy staff members. A few serve as counselors to ministers and their families in denominationally sponsored programs. A considerable number teach counseling in seminaries. Several seminaries now offer doctoral programs in pastoral psychology and counseling to prepare specialists.

er in continuing education programs in counseling and pastoral care.

An illustration of a clinically based training course is one which is offered at the Lutheran Social Service Center in Minneapolis. Many who take this course are pastors who have had previous clinical training. Ordinarily, the course is full time for twelve weeks, or 480 hours; some pastors enroll for six months with twenty-hour weeks. The interprofessional staff of the agency—including social workers, clinical psychologists, a consulting psychiatrist, and an accredited chaplain supervisor who directs and coordinates the training—share the teaching responsibilities. One day a week is set aside for instruction, guest lecturers, teaching seminar, visiting other institutions, etc. A minimum of one hour per week is spent in individual supervision, focusing on the cases with whom each student is counseling (particularly marriage counseling), to increase the minister's competence as a parish pastor. For some it is a part of training for specialized ministries of pastoral counseling.

Another example of clinically based continuing education is a pastoral counseling center related to a seminary. The staff of this center is composed of clergymen who have had clinical training and of graduate students in pastoral counseling. The parish ministers receive supervision of their counseling with parishioners. Some also do counseling at the center, as do the graduate students. Supervision is provided by two faculty persons in the pastoral care field and by a panel of three psychiatrists who rotate every three months. A four-hour training session attended by the full staff includes case presentations by two trainees, an hour and a half with the psychiatrist, viewing of a videotape of a counseling session, and a period when the theological dimension of clients' problems are explored. Each staff member is expected to counsel four hours per week, which often includes participating as a co-leader of a counseling group. Ministers and graduate students are expected to remain on the center's staff for at least nine months. During this time most of them receive supervised experience in individual, couple, conjoint family, and group counseling. This center operates as both a clinical training base and a service arm of the local Council of Churches. The latter provides space and secretarial assistance in making appointments.

Another model of the use of a clinical setting for clergy training in pastoral marriage counseling was developed at Marriage Council of Philadelphia.

This program was a one-day-a-week program for a group of seven Catholic priests from a New Jersey diocese. Co-leaders were two priests who are teachers at Maryknoll Seminary and who had been participants in the NIMH program. The group met each Wednesday from 9:30 A.M. to 6:30 P.M. for approximately two months. The morning session focused on family dynamics and marriage counseling theory. This was followed by a case conference (in which one priest presented a case each week), peer group supervision, and then individual supervision. In their evaluation the participants identified many positive aspects of the program: experience in reality-oriented counseling; the clarification of theory as applied to and derived from actual cases with whom they were counseling; learning to be aware of the counselor's role and the interaction between counselor and client; observing a live interview by a staff member, which helped in learning a more active use of self in counseling. All the priests felt that the program should have been longer, because they felt they were gaining so much.

Informal Supervision and Growth Groups

Two forms of continuing education which have proved to be rapid growth stimulators for ministers are supervision groups and growth groups. These have the advantage of being available in any location where there is a competent clinician. They can be set up by counseling agencies of all kinds and by clergymen themselves taking the initiative in assembling a group and arranging for a trained leader-supervisor. The leader may be a specialist in pastoral counseling, a clinically trained chaplain, or a member of one of the mental health professions. The mushrooming network of comprehensive community mental health programs offers an excellent new resource for consultation services with clergy groups.

Ordinarily the purpose of a group is either supervision or the personal professional growth of the ministers. There is, however, always an overlapping of these two functions. Dynamic supervision involves the minister's as well as the parishioner's side of the counseling relationship. Good supervision is a growth experience. Conversely, ministers' growth groups frequently focus on hang-ups with parishioners, including counselees. An example follows:

One intensive growth group involved an interdenominational group of eight ministers. They met for a "self-other awareness" group each morning for three hours, on four successive days. Various nonverbal methods were utilized at the beginning of each session.[9] These tended to produce heightened awareness of feelings and rapid movement by the group to a level of significant interaction. The leader, a clinically trained pastoral counselor, served as process facilitator; his efforts were directed at helping the members experience their feelings and relationships, communicate more effectively and honestly, and focus on what was actually occurring in the group. He was to be as aware and transparent as possible with respect to his own humanness and feelings.

The ministers confronted each other and themselves. They shared their frustrations about the ministry, their marriages, and the problems in many of their other relationships. In the evaluation at the end of the last day, one of the men expressed feelings that seemed to be common: "I've gotten acquainted with my wall and even broken through it at times in this group. I feel I really know you fellows for the first time, even though most of us have been associating for several years. My loneliness has taken a beating here." There was general agreement that they wanted to have a similar experience in a group with their wives.

A growth group experience is continuing education in the broad sense of enhancing a minister's ability to use

[9] These methods are described in William C. Schutz, *Joy: Expanding Human Awareness* (New York: Grove Press, 1967).

himself, his skills, and his knowledge in his professional relationships. To the extent that it improves his awareness and effectiveness in relationships, it will make him a more effective counselor. The following example stresses the minister's family relationship:

A seminary-sponsored growth group for husbands and wives met once a week for fifteen weeks. It was led by a seminary teacher of pastoral counseling and his wife, a social worker. The group consisted of seven couples; four of the husbands were clergymen and three theological students. The purpose of the group was defined as "the deepening of marital relationships through increase in the ability to communicate and relate in mutually satisfying ways." The group used nonverbal sensitivity training methods as well as verbal interaction. Couples focused on their own and each other's relationships and on their feelings and problems with respect to the ministry. The purpose of the group seemed to be realized, at least to a limited degree, in each of the couples; several had breakthrough experiences in communicating. Besides deepening their marriages, participants found themselves functioning more effectively professionally.

Still another type of group—a supervision group—is illustrated by the following example:

This group was set up in a pastoral counseling center in a downtown church (First Methodist) in Pasadena, California. Six ministers and one director of religious education met once a week for two and a half hours. The announced purpose was to offer an opportunity for help with one's pastoral counseling problems. As rapport developed within the group, the ministers began to discuss administrative difficulties and the attacks from reactionary laymen within their churches. Insights from pastoral psychology and counseling were related to noncounseling aspects of their work. Some newer methods of family life education were discussed and demonstrated by the leader. This group was structured so as to terminate after ten weeks. Similar groups have continued in an open-ended way for a year or more, adding new members as others drop out or move from the area.

Common Ingredients in Effective Patterns

There are five ingredients which appear repeatedly in effective patterns of continuing education: *conceptual tool enrichment, case supervision, skill practice, self-awareness experiences,* and *pastoral teaching and supervision.* Acquiring new ways of understanding marital interaction—for example, to grasp the meaning of Eric Berne's Parent/Adult/ Child approach to understanding interpersonal transactions —can be useful to a counseling pastor. Experience has shown, however, that theoretical material is most meaningful when it meets the practical need of the counselor for understanding and helping a particular person or couple. This is why beginning with case material is often the most fruitful way to approach continuing education in counseling.

Faced by the heavy interpersonal demands of their ministry, pastors are highly receptive to useful conceptual tools but rejecting of "irrelevant theory." Direct supervision of a clergyman's counseling is one of the most efficient ways to enhance his interpersonal skills. Interprofessional team supervision is highly desirable, but it is essential that at least one competent person with a firm ministerial identity do part of the supervision. Each profession is a kind of subculture with its own symbols, language, lore, myths, identity, and self-image. The professional identity of clergymen becomes diffused, and even confused, if all their dynamic learning experiences in continuing education are with persons from the other counseling professions. The pastoral teacher and supervisor speaks the language of the minister because he knows this profession from the inside. He therefore has a unique function in the process of helping a fellow minister firm up his professional self-esteem and identity through continuing education. It is especially important that clergy-supervisors be involved in the small group experiences in which the goals are increased awareness of one's self and one's relationships.

In his book *Education and Ecstasy,* George Leonard sets forth his vision of the role of education in the world of tomorrow: "Education in a new and broadened sense can become a lifelong pursuit for everyone. To go on learning, to go on sharing that learning with others may well be considered a purpose worthy of mankind's ever-expanding capacities." [10] Ministers should be among those who first

[10] P. 16.

embrace this style of lifelong learning with enthusiasm. Through a pattern of continuing education, with a strong emphasis on supervision, they can stay equipped to nurture the continuing growth of their people, by continuing to grow themselves.